89 - 0434

The Darkness We Carry

The Darkness We Carry
The Drama of the Holocaust

ROBERT SKLOOT

The University of Wisconsin Press

Published 1988

The University of Wisconsin Press
114 North Murray Street
Madison, Wisconsin 53715

The University of Wisconsin Press, Ltd.
1 Gower Street
London WC1E 6HA, England

First printing

Printed in the United States of America

For LC CIP information see the colophon

ISBN 0-299-11660-3 cloth; 0-299-11664-6 paper

Chapter 1 first appeared in a slightly different form in *New Theatre Quarterly* III,
(November 1987) and is reprinted with permission of Cambridge University Press
and the Editors of *New Theatre Quarterly*.

Again, for
JoAnn, Sarah, and Julia

All of us obviously have something in common. We do tend to recognize one another whenever we meet, nearly at a glance, by some common trick of feeling, by the darkness we carry. But each of us must hammer it out for himself.

—George Steiner
"A Kind of Survivor"

Contents

Introduction

*T*HE following is an unpublished play consisting of a single scene, if such a simple piece of dialogue and description can be called a play. It was sent to me by a Polish friend, an elderly professor and survivor of the Bialystok Ghetto and the concentration camps, whom I met in Warsaw in 1978. Learning of my interest in the drama of the Holocaust, he told me of the death of his wife and two little daughters during those terrible years. Some months later I received this letter from him.

Warsaw, 25 I 1979

Dear Professor Skloot,

I thank you for your remembering my little [granddaughter] Ruth and for sending her the little white shirt to her 1st anniversary of her birthday. The little one is an amiable sunny creature. When—*b'ezrat Hashem* [with God's help]—grown up she will be told about her friends in the distant Madison, Wisc., and she will thank for herself.

I would like to reciprocate for your being so kind. A propos the Holocaust studied by you.

I'll try to give you if no some inspiration so some idea. (Introduction): Bialystok-Ghetto, winter (January) 1943, before an "action," feverish preparation to save the life, dug outs, hidings and . . . buying drugs for the little ones, they must sleep when the gang will enter and seek victims for Treblinka, they shall not wake up and cry and so betray the hiding . . . Soon, as usually, on the market appeared falsified drugs without any value . . .

(Act IV): Father: Have you the stuff?
        Seller: Well . . .
        F: Don't be afraid. I know you have it. But I must be sure. Is it real? Will it work?
        S: It will. It's excellent.
        F: I hope so. Pain?
        S: No pain.
        F: Will sleep?

S: Like a young angel.
F: I don't care about angels. It is for my beloved
          son, my only one . . .

It remains only to write the 1st, 2nd, 3rd, and 5th act and only
to begin and finish the 4th one. Think it over for yourself or
together with your students. Not every word of the above is true
but the story is true. I can add for the use of the playwriter: The
boy then escaped, but a 4 year old sunny girl, Baziunia, did not.
She awoke when the Germans entered the room and she began to
cry. One professor of mathematics, a decent man, put his hand on
her neck, certainly he wished not to kill her. I buried the little
blond angel in the garden under the room where was hiding. The
mother of the little angel stretched through the window to me her
tiny body. I remember her last words. Look, maybe she is still
alive. But she wasn't. It was a moony mild winter night, but the
soil was hard, it was difficult to dig a grave.
          I wish you all the best

P.S. Excuse me the story and my English

The Darkness We Carry is a belated response to this friend's letter.
          For more than ten years, much of my professional and personal life
has been occupied with the study of the Holocaust. Most people whose
"lives" coincide so auspiciously would be counted fortunate and, to a
degree, I am. But it would be incorrect to say that mine is happy work,
for the subject under scrutiny often places me at the mercy of the grim-
mest of materials. My family lost no one in the Holocaust, but the horrible events created a demand on my attention impossible to resist. I am
sure this involvement is due largely to my Jewishness, although I recognize that many Jews remain rather unconcerned with the Holocaust,
and others, at the woeful other extreme, have made it an obsession
resulting in excessively narrow self-definition. Certainly, I am drawn
to reflect on the Holocaust for the ethical, cultural, and aesthetic problems it encompasses, although I am mindful also of the theological or
political issues it subsumes under its insatiable shadow.
          In this book, whose title comes from the essay "A Kind of Survivor"
by George Steiner, I have tried to further explore my thoughts about
and responses to the Holocaust and to Holocaust drama that I described initially in the introduction to *The Theatre of the Holocaust*
(1982). The twenty-five plays discussed in the following chapters appeared over a period of thirty years. The attitudes they reflect cover a

wide range of feelings about the Holocaust and its legacy. Since the mid-1950s, an increasing number of plays have dealt with Holocaust issues and, taken as a group, they are an enormously varied lot in form and content. Their differences result from many factors, including the age, nationality, gender, language, sexual preference, or political bias of the playwright. The forms they take are striking in their diversity while they all deal with the same historical event. A collection of several of these plays might be assembled only to display their individual styles: American melodrama (Goodrich and Hackett's *The Diary of Anne Frank*), English black comedy (Barnes's *Laughter!*), French realism (Grumberg's *The Workroom*), Israeli epic theatre (Sobol's *Ghetto*), European theatre of cruelty (Tabori's *The Cannibals*), and German documentary drama (Weiss's *The Investigation*). Taken separately, each of these plays is inadequate to the task of explaining the Holocaust; as a group, they, along with the other plays discussed in this volume, give a better (although still partial) picture of what the Holocaust was like and what its contemporary significance is when re-created in the imaginations of playwrights.

To all these plays I have tried to apply a double measure by seeing them as both moral texts and theatrical events. The plays that succeed in both realms, in vision and in practice, are the ones I believe should be counted among the major artistic achievements of Holocaust drama or, indeed, of twentieth-century drama in general. In many cases, plays succeed in one area but not in the other. In a few cases, a play will fail in both ways, but my interest in it is to explore the reasons for the failure. I believe that plays considering serious subjects possess an ethical aspect or function, and nowhere is this more keenly seen than in Holocaust drama. Consequently, I have tried to be especially clear, in my analyses, about my own ethical and aesthetic biases on the way to reaching judgment.

Among the plays under discussion, many are well known, and a few are relatively unknown but deserve greater popular attention. (None of them will ever be popular if by that word we mean that it must have a large following of enthusiastic audiences; the dramatization of Anne Frank's diary is the exception to this condition.) That status is denied to Holocaust drama for reasons almost too obvious to mention. Simply, the common event that unites all these plays is the most terrifying and incomprehensible episode in modern times. The presentation of the Holocaust in the public forum of the theatre can summon up an attitude of "why do I have to see that kind of horrible stuff?" Most theatregoers are not inclined to attend one of these plays when deciding about an evening out at the theatre (unless there is a "star" involved), a situation that only enhances the obligation to force a confrontation with these texts. Even the best of them are produced less frequently than they should be. In truth, one of the objectives of this book of essays is to stimulate producers and directors, especially in America, to consider staging dramas of the Holocaust, and to help them find the "right" script. (I will not discuss the new television form, the star-filled Holocaust miniseries, which, with melodramatic story, upbeat ending, and commercial interruption, has made its special contribution to the compromising of Holocaust memory and the cheapening of Holocaust history under the guise of "serious entertainment.")

But as so many commentators have noted, the Holocaust is also a painful subject that is easily, perhaps willfully, forgotten, and breaking the silence that threatens to engulf it is an important motivator in producing these plays. When it is broken, however, the sounds we hear (and the images we see) must be clearly and responsibly enunciated. Even then, as with any theatre production, countless problems may occur; it makes sense to prepare for as many of them as possible. The work that needs to be done to reduce the awful ignorance of the Holocaust, now more than forty years past, is easily and sometimes accidentally sabotaged.

There are two other reasons why this material engages me. First, the Holocaust in the theatre presents problems that are different than those found in prose or poetry, film or music, and they deserve discussion. The theatre possesses an immediacy and impact which surpasses all the other art forms. There is a condition inherently exciting in the work of live actors creating characters before us on stage in a public forum, and the relationship between actor and audience is potentially more moving, certainly more volatile. In so many of the plays discussed in this book, a crucial moment occurs when the actors *acknowledge the audience* in some fashion; often this is the moment that reveals the playwright's point of view. Further, if those actors are playing characters named Chaim Rumkowski or Jacob Gens, Janusz Korczak or Adolf Hitler, an additional provocative dimension is added to the theatrical event, for history is coming alive before us and it demands our intellectual as well as our emotional response.

Second, by working with this material and judging its effectiveness and significance, I acknowledge that this material exists and deserves critical attention. This is, in itself, a refutation of the often-repeated claim that the artistic imagination is inferior to the historical event or presumes too much when it engages the historical experience. Many critics argue that artists should display more humility, restraint, and "taste" when dealing with this subject; others call for an end to commercial exploitation of the Holocaust. Nonetheless, because artists are not known for their reticence, and because individual perspectives and competences should be evaluated on a case-by-case basis, the plays brought together in this book, representing all forms and points of view about the Holocaust, call out for critical response. In addition, these discussions help to maintain the Holocaust itself in the public's attention.

I have gathered the plays together under headings that I find useful for analysis. Other critics have looked at Holocaust drama from other directions and reached different conclusions about some of the texts. But with an ethical-theatrical bias to guide me, I have chosen the following distribution, one which permits coherence and flexibility. (*Throne of Straw*, for example, is discussed in three chapters from differing perspectives; *Brother Eichmann*, discussed under the category of German-language drama, is also relevant to the issue of interchangeability of identities remarked upon elsewhere in the book.)

In chapter 1, I discuss the relationship of two issues crucial to understanding the Holocaust and its theatrical interpretation: survival and choice. In chapter 2, I explore the idea of tragedy and how the traditional beliefs surrounding this kind of writing have been rejected or reconciled to the materials from history the Holocaust provides. Chapter 3 presents a discussion of how the comic and tragicomic forms have been used by playwrights, and chapter 4 investigates how several playwrights have chosen to theatricalize the Holocaust by writing plays that involve the transfer of identities between Jewish victims and Nazi oppressors. In the fifth chapter, I review a selection of plays in the German-language theatre that span a generation of experience in confronting (or avoiding) the Holocaust. Finally, in chapter 6, I draw together several conclusions about theatrical form, content, and intention and, applying them to two controversial artistic treatments of the Holocaust, one play and one film, discuss the responsibilities of artists and audiences.

Working with the drama of the Holocaust, part of what Lawrence Langer calls "the literature of atrocity," is something I do because it is the best way to continue asking necessary questions that present no clear answers. In plays of the Holocaust we can see images placed before our eyes from a time in history that, at least for most of us, has passed. We see a landscape of horror and humiliation re-created by live human beings; if it is created with integrity and presented with skill, that is, without sentimentality and free from political or pornographic exploitation, it can move us to ponder the great issues that the distractions of a more mundane existence usually prevent us from considering. At their most basic, the plays, in their various styles, describe an immense intellectual and emotional territory all of us inhabit. Within that landscape—defined at one extreme by the theatricalized Anne Frank with her youthful, unavailing optimism, and on the other by the mature and death-laden pragmatism of George Tabori's SS man—we search for understanding of the Holocaust. We can never know enough about this territory, and although its mysteries are permanent, this is the space where Holocaust testimony and Holocaust drama tell us we must live some of the time to learn more about ourselves and the world.

The following people and institutions deserve acknowledgment for the assistance and encouragement given me on the long road to the completion of this book: Kenneth Bernard, Ted Bourns, Harry Cargas, Ron Carson, Szymon Datner, Anat Feinberg, the Graduate School of the University of Wisconsin–Madison, Gary Heisserer, Ted Herstand, Lawrence Langer, Sara Markham, Merope Pavlides, Mike Phayer, Alvin Rosenfeld, Irv Saposnik, Ellen Schiff, and Mary Zellmer. If there are faults with my work, I ask their pardon for "my story and my English."

The Darkness We Carry

One

Choice and/or Survival

This event is a wound that will not heal; even the balm of intelligibility is denied to us.

—Susan Sontag

SURELY most Europeans and Americans are familiar with at least a few powerful images of the Holocaust: desperate families with hands raised being deported by smiling German soldiers, frightened children evacuating an airless boxcar, stiff-looking partisans posing in a forest clearing, vacant-eyed concentration camp inmates staring through barbed wire, hills of degraded, decomposed bodies. These images, and dozens more like them, have become part of the iconography of our modern civilization, a visual reminder of those years, only a generation ago, when Nazi evil nearly usurped humanity's dominion in its attempt to destroy Europe's Jewish population. They come to us by way of photographs and films, and provide documentary evidence, in visceral terms, of what was lost to the world and what survived. This chapter seeks to describe how the theatre (as distinct from movies and television) creates and uses images of the Holocaust in a complex, urgent attempt to bring to life the dark time of our recent past. Because those images inevitably involve an attempt to understand the subjects of survival and continuance, this chapter, after addressing several "theories of survival," relates to those theories a number of representative plays

This essay was written at the invitation of the Institute for the Medical Humanities of the University of Texas Medical Branch, Galveston, Texas, and presented in a somewhat different form at the "Making Sense of Survival" Research Seminar, November 15–16, 1984, Galveston, Texas.

dealing with the experience of the Holocaust's victims whose fate is influenced by the choices they make regarding survival.

I

For more than forty years, Bruno Bettelheim has maintained a keen and controversial interest in the Holocaust and its relationship to survival; his longevity and prolificacy have accorded him a status that few other commentators on the Holocaust have received. In 1979, a number of his essays on the subject were collected into a volume called *Surviving,* and in that book we can locate his often-expressed central concerns. As early as 1943, with the war in Europe raging, Bettelheim published an essay, "Individual and Mass Behavior in Extreme Situations," in which he describes the breakdown of the autonomous personality under the depredations of concentration camp life. At the end of the essay he sets out the purpose of the tyrant's system and the antidote to its successful operation.

> The main goal of the Nazi effort seemed to be to produce in their subjects childlike attitudes and childlike dependency on the will of the leaders. The most effective way to break this influence seemed to be the formation of democratic resistance groups of independent, mature, and self-reliant persons, in which every member backed up, in all other members, the ability to resist.[1]

Bettelheim's interest, from the first, lay in elaborating upon a type of behavior which would accord the individual in an extreme situation a dignity without which survival would be meaningless. He asserts that a certain line must not be crossed if we are to maintain our personal integrity. Once the line is overstepped, we forsake our claim to membership in a mutually supportive and creative human enterprise and (most controversially) *participate in our own destruction.* For Bruno Bettelheim, the key to a survival that is more than just organic continuance lies in exercising the *choice* to resist oppression, behavior that is supported by a sociocultural apparatus that lends strength to individual action.

Over the years, Bettelheim has continually emphasized the importance of the survivor's experience *for us.* In essays written between 1963 ("Eichmann: The System, the Victims") and 1977 ("The Holocaust—One Generation Later"), Bettelheim writes of "the warning it holds for man today," stressing that the survivor of the concentration camps can teach us a lesson that we forget at our peril. Without the warning, "thoughtful men are closed off from valid insights into what attitudes we must develop to prevent it all from ever happening again."[2] It is just this sort of prophetic posture that has augmented Bettelheim's stature as a commentator on the Holocaust, combining as it does his own experience in Dachau in the 1930s, his forthright concern to keep alive the memory of the millions of victims, and his exceedingly rational —even programmatic—understanding of the lessons we must learn. Positive individual action becomes both representative and symbolic of the options available to all of us in "extreme situations," but only if we have the courage and will to engage in them, says Bettelheim. In those "times of trouble," of Treblinka or Hiroshima, our charge is to jump the tracks of our mundane concerns to the more exalted road of heroic action and meaningful commitment. Doing this involves the crucial choice of willing our continuation as rational, purposeful, pragmatic people; failure leads to degradation and paralysis, which have little to distinguish them from actual, physical extinction.

In another view, however, Bettelheim's understanding and recommendations are inherently wrong, because they specify a belief in individual action that can oppose powerful, tyrannical social-political forces with some chance of success. The error of Bettelheim's theory, which is more than a rejection of his dogmatic style, is that its historical premise is not wholly accurate and its romantic, narrow assumptions lead to a mean-spiritedness that attaches itself to an evaluation of character. The latter is nowhere more evident than in his essay "The Ignored Lesson of Anne Frank," (1960) where he approaches too closely (in tone if not in argument) the position of "blaming the victims" by criticizing the Franks not merely for denying reality and forsaking escape, but implicitly for not providing us (the reader or viewer) with a clear *image* of resistance. ("But Anne, her sister, her mother, may well have died because her parents could not get themselves to believe in Auschwitz."[3]) It is a reproach with important implications for Bettelheim's aesthetic judgment as well. (See chapter 6.)

Bettelheim's eloquent antagonist in the critical debate over characters in Holocaust history and art is Terrence Des Pres, author of *The Survivor: An Anatomy of Life in the Death Camps.* Since that book's publication in 1976, Des Pres and Bettelheim have written opposing and often angry evaluations of each other's work, a confrontation that exploded that same year in their public argument over Lina Wertmuller's film *Seven Beauties.*[4] One value of *The Survivor,* one perhaps more irksome to Bettelheim than to others, lies in Des Pres's demythologizing the concentration camp experience through an em-

phasis on the *quietness,* even *humility,* of the survivor's behavior. In his
chapter "Nightmare and Waking," Des Pres writes of a crucial moment
in the life of the survivor.

> They turned to face the worst straight-on, without sentiment or
> special hope, simply to keep watch over life. And when the mo-
> ment of turning came, finally, it was attended by a strong sensa-
> tion of choice, a feeling of new determination, as if the decision to
> survive were an inner fate expressing itself through a conscious as-
> sent of the will. . . . That is the moment of waking, of return; and
> this book, as I write, enacts the same resolution, the same kind of
> turn—away from the monstrous inhumanity of the concentration
> camps, away from the despair and nihilism they authorize, back to
> the small strands of life and decency which constitute, however
> faint and scattered, a fabric of discernible goodness amid that evil.[5]

In Des Pres, we find little of the need to envision an emblematic,
even mythic, meaning for survival; in his concentration on the details
of continuance guided by a biological as well as a volitional energy and
uninformed by a didactic appeal to the larger structures or
psychological needs of human experience, Des Pres extracts findings
different than Bettelheim's from the same history and reduces the
latter's heroic vision. In extreme situations, we need not jump tracks,
only continue "steady in our humanness" in Des Pres's words; "the moment of turning" is described as restorative and reflective, community
oriented, naturally undertaken. Whatever else can be said in comparing
these two writers, they reveal opposing personalities and outlooks.
Bettelheim's posture is authoritarian, aristocratic, and romantic; Des
Pres's is spiritual, contemplative, and realistically proletarian. And like
the realists in literature a century ago, who fought against *their* romantic ancestors over a truer understanding of the meaning of life, Des Pres
finds heroism in the smallest of actions; "their victories were never
large," he writes.[6] In a response to Bettelheim's attack on him, Des Pres
asserts: "when we think of existence in Auschwitz, the fact that many
men and women survived by keeping their humanity intact seems extraordinary to the point of heroism."[7]

One part of the argument between these two writers provides a
bridge into a discussion of the drama of the Holocaust. In his book,
Des Pres describes "a strong sensation of choice" that accompanied
"the moment of turning" of the concentration camp prisoner. Des Pres
explores this further: ". . . even to accomplish victories so small, so apparently insignificant against defeats so appalling, they must make

choices painful, often past bearing. Many could not bear it. They chose to die, rather than survive on such terms."[8] This is a crucial point of overlap between the two critics since apparently we all face moments of choice in extreme situations, even the most unworthy of us. In the essays in *Surviving,* Bettelheim is equally emphatic about this kind of behavior. For example, he seeks a lesson not only from the Frank family's decision to hide in an attic, "to examine first whether it was a reasonable or an effective choice,"[9] but also from Adolf Eichmann who experienced (and failed) his test at the "moment of choice" when he confronted his Jewish victims face-to-face for the first time. Bettelheim defines this moment as the point when "an individual [is] still able to save his soul and perhaps also his life."[10]

Nonetheless, there is much disagreement among survivors and commentators concerning survival and its relationship to this moment of choice. For example, in his essay "Postscript" (1966), George Steiner, one of the most illuminating critics of modern European culture and literature, adduces the great value of Jean-François Steiner's concentration camp memoir, *Treblinka:* ". . . he makes one grasp something of a deliberate torture of hope and choice by which the Nazis broke the spring of will in men." To go on living "almost invariably involved a choice so hideous, so degrading that it further diminished the humanity of those who made it. . . . To live was to choose to become less human."[11]

The crucial idea here is George Steiner's linkage of survival in the death camps to hope and choice, and how the latter two were diminished when each *mutually degraded* the other. Although these conditions prevailed after the war's official start in 1939, Steiner remarks on Bettelheim's prewar camp experience (also noted critically by Des Pres) as one where normal (i.e., noncamp) options and behaviors still obtained, although the conditions of imprisonment were highly dangerous and behavior much constrained. His point here, and in the essay to which his remarks are a postscript, is that the world created by the Nazis for the Jews was unimaginable before it occurred and remains almost equally so today. Steiner's essay also concludes that what is imagined and imaginable *is directly related* to the attitude we take toward survival one generation after the Holocaust.

There are numerous works of Holocaust literature and drama that focus on the survivor who seeks to salvage some viable form of human existence despite the relentless onslaught of the oppressor. Several literary works of this kind are studied under the heading "Literature of Survival" in Sidra DeKoven Ezrahi's book *By Words Alone: The Holo-*

caust in Literature. In assessing the achievement of selected writers, Ezrahi concludes that the survivor of this type of novel is "one who resists his condition as a victim." Later she writes:

> The ability to accommodate ambiguous and relative attitudes without relinquishing a moral code altogether seems to have been the single most important factor in determining the quality, if not the duration, of survival in the concentrationary universe.[12]

What is interesting in Ezrahi's analysis is her gathering together examples of Holocaust literature that combine Des Pres's understanding of the death camp world with the type of behavior that Bettelheim prefers and champions. Her remark that certain Holocaust writers show that "in the end, the rebel may not succeed in preserving his own life, but at least he will not have become an accomplice to the murder of others," is entirely consistent with Bettelheim's desire for pragmatic images of Holocaust behavior. Still, she reduces the images of heroism in the "literature of survival" to "the minimal gestures of self-preservation."[13] In her keenly observed discussion, Ezrahi may have unknowingly uncovered the true source of antagonism between Bettelheim and Des Pres: an irreconcilable disagreement over the *use* to which the literature of the Holocaust can be put. In any case, Ezrahi pinpoints and discusses the crucial issue of the Holocaust concerning survival: can mere survival be a sufficient and a sufficiently positive result of the Nazis' attempt to destroy all Jews? Or are there other qualities of survivorship that must be considered before we can evaluate the true nature of the survivor's condition? The relationship of these questions to the issues of choice is neither accidental nor superficial, and what it tells us about the ethical premises of playwrights of Holocaust drama is very important.

Among the most uncompromising commentators on the Holocaust and theories of survival is Lawrence Langer, whose works have strongly influenced readers of Holocaust literature, including myself. In his most recent book, *Versions of Survival: The Holocaust and the Human Spirit* (1982), Langer directly attacks the central premise of both Bettelheim and Des Pres; from his reading of history and survivors' memoirs, he follows Steiner in arguing that not only was human choice nearly impossible in the camps, it was morally repugnant as an option even when possible: ". . . the Nazi mind created a world where meaningful choice disappeared and the hope for survival was made to depend on equally impossible alternatives."[14] He relentlessly leads us back to the conditions of moral confusion that the perpetrators of the evil fashioned for their victims. In addition, he is resolute in a desire to supply the victims with the dignity which has often been denied them.

> But the human imagination has been nourished for so long on such abstractions that it continues to relish them and prefer them to the less savory options of moral confusion or despair, or to the more indigestible diet of learning to live with a double vision and speak with two voices—the voice of Auschwitz and the voice of civilization. . . . In the camps themselves, few were free to *do* even what they thought or felt; they did what they must, to stay alive, with a vague sense that the most crucial choices were not theirs at all.[15]

Not surprisingly, Langer is angered by Bettelheim and is sharp in his attack on him. He accuses Bettelheim of romanticism and condescension in his inability or refusal to envision the victims of the Holocaust, whether survivors or not, in an utterly degraded world that permitted *no* opportunity for moral choice or hope. Langer is approving of Des Pres, but rejects his conclusions about survival because although Des Pres *sees* correctly the condition of life in the camps, he nonetheless postulates a program or strategy that, in general, makes meaningful survival a certain degree more possible. "Gratitude that some tens of thousands survived while millions died should not be mistaken for a principle of redemptive meaning."[16] In his chapter "Auschwitz: The Death of Choice," Langer reflects upon the victims with a concern and caring that give his uncompromisingly pessimistic discussion a moral bias of its own:

> . . . how little discredit falls to these victims, who were plunged into a crisis of what we might call "choiceless choice," where crucial decisions did not reflect options between life and death, but between one form of abnormal response and another, both imposed by a situation that was in no way of the victim's own choosing.[17]

Langer's thinking on this subject is guided in part by the Polish critic Andrzej Wirth who, in 1967, published an essay on the life and short stories of Tadeusz Borowski titled "A Discovery of Tragedy." Wirth locates the heart of classical tragedy in the clash of two irreconcilable opposites, using the model of Sophocles' *Antigone* as the standard against which Borowski's "new" vision of tragedy can be compared. Because inside the "criminal world" of concentration camps the opportunity for "individualistic, exemplary" behavior was impossible, the deliberate commitment to a fate or value was rendered useless, he writes. Despite the fact that Borowski wrote prose (not plays), and that

there are other models of tragedy that offer themselves for a more
useful study of the Holocaust experience in the theatre (see chapter 2),
Wirth does make the crucial point about the matter of choice.

> The hero of Borowski's stories is a hero *deprived of all choice*. He
> finds himself in a situation without choice because every choice is
> base. The tragedy lies not in the necessity of choosing but in the
> impossibility of making a choice. The emergencies of such situa-
> tions, whose inhumanity lies in their lack of any alternative,
> Borowski describes as characteristic of the new times.[18]

This is the bleak condition that Steiner first identified and discussed in
his essays from the 1960s. In the 1980s, Steiner again addressed the
paradoxes and conundrums of the Holocaust in a short novel that was
dramatized by Christopher Hampton as *George Steiner's The Portage
to San Cristobal of A.H.*,[19] which I will discuss later in this book.

II

In the introduction to *The Theatre of the Holocaust*, a 1982 anthology of plays on the Holocaust theme, I listed five objectives of
serious playwrights who are drawn to this forbidding part of our recent
history: honoring the victims, teaching history to audiences, evoking
emotional responses, discussing ethical issues, and suggesting solutions
to universal, contemporary problems.[20] To a large degree, achieving
these philosophical, epideictic, didactic, or theatrical objectives
depends on the capacity for *symbolizing*, on finding the appropriate
metaphor to carry the performance to a satisfactory conclusion. The
aesthetic issues here concern the dramatist's vision of the Holocaust
survivor as representative of humanity, and the means by which this
connection is achieved on stage. Usually, the survivor is a Jew. In her
discussion of images of Jews in the theatre, *From Stereotype to Metaphor*, Ellen Schiff writes: "In an impressive number of contemporary
situations, the experience of the Jew is viewed as a comprehensive
experience, and the figure of the Jew comes to stand as a metaphor for
modern mankind."[21] Schiff remarks cogently on the stage image of the
Jew as revolutionary, as outsider, and as ethical standard, among
others. I would advance an additional characteristic based on survivorship: the ambiguous image of the Jew as Carrier of Darkness.

It is possible and useful to suggest that Jews and images of Jews are
attractive to people for both their suffering and their continuance. Jewish experience provides individuals and peoples with the image of the
survivor, and it is this image that playwrights have available to use for

their various objectives. In the Holocaust context, the experience of the survivor can be analyzed and dramatized. Steiner has even written of the Nazis' need to "kill the remembrancer," to eradicate along with the Jews themselves something that Jews carry inside them that serves as a permanent rebuke to the murderers and a continuous reminder of the long-term failure of their purpose.[22] In a passage from his novel *The Town Beyond the Wall,* Elie Wiesel articulates a similar idea:

> If all nations, in the long course of history, have taken bitter pains to trample on the Jews, it is perhaps because they wished to know that strange people who, more than any other, possess the secret of survival, the key to the mystery of time, the formula for endurance.[23]

The obvious evidence of continuance, together with the millennial depredations of history, form the material that can make survivorship serve as theatrical and existential paradigm. But as has been noted in the earlier discussion of survival in the Holocaust, the truth this material carries is neither easily controlled nor universally accepted.

In a definite way, our understanding Holocaust history as well as Holocaust drama depends on our understanding the nature of the victims' choice presented to the audience. Conventional wisdom, historical and social, indicates that without exercising choice we cannot insure survival; theatrical wisdom insists that without dramatizing choice we can have no theatre, certainly not in the ways we are used to knowing it. And popular sentiment, as well as individual need for a sense of a dignified and autonomous selfhood, causes us to resist mightily images that seek to deny our ability to exercise some control over life's conditions.[24] For these reasons, "positive" Holocaust plays, inspirational and didactic, appear most popular on the stage. But, seen from the perspective of Langer, Steiner, and perhaps Des Pres, the premises on which they are based contain historical and aesthetic falsehoods.

The playwrights of the Holocaust are thus confronted with certain artistic choices of their own. They need to establish clearly their own understanding of history and, equally clearly, to describe their understanding of what survival means in the context of that history. Their images of survival do this. When dramatized, certain individual viewpoints can be established: whether survival is possible under the conditions shown, whether it results from human effort or accident, whether it is worthwhile. To audiences who seek insight into the issues of continuance, belief, and hope in a post-Holocaust world, these viewpoints, when precisely expressed in theatrical images, have great power and authority. Ezrahi writes that: "the representation of the Holocaust in art is, essentially, an oscillation and a struggle between continuity and discontinuity with the cultural as well as with the historical past."[25]

III

The four plays anthologized in *The Theatre of the Holocaust* provide useful material for a discussion of how survivorship is dramatized for the stage. Taken together, the many images of survivors share characteristics that tell us much about how modern playwrights attempt to make sense out of survival in the context of the Holocaust experience. Importantly, the four plays address the question of human choice, and do so not only for historical but for dramatic reasons. In addition, the decisions the playwrights make as to *where* to set their plays also bear importantly on the issue of survival and choice.

Throne of Straw (1978), by Harold and Edith Lieberman, is set in the city of Lodz, Poland, during the years 1939 to 1944. It tells the story of the destruction of the Jews of Lodz, who, before the war, comprised about 40 percent of the city's population of seven hundred thousand. The protagonist of the play is Mordechai Chaim Rumkowski,[26] who was appointed head of the *Judenrat* (the Jewish council) by the German occupiers; Rumkowski presided over the incorporation and subsequent destruction of the Balut section of the city, which was established as the ever more degraded Jewish ghetto. For arranging the transports to the death camps and deciding who was to be the human cargo, Rumkowski earned his reputation as an efficient and ruthless collaborator; yet, he truly believed himself to be another savior of the Jewish people. The last Jews of Lodz, unlike the Jews of Warsaw a year earlier, did not overtly or collectively resist the Germans, and they were destroyed. Rumkowski, the "Elder" of Lodz, appears to have made the wrong moral choices in administering the ghetto's rise and fall.

(There is a grim historical irony in Rumkowski's assumption, which the Liebermans emphasize in their play. In the summer of 1944, although Lodz was reduced in Jewish population to between sixty and seventy thousand, Rumkowski, in league with the Nazi administrator Biebow, was in charge of the largest remnant of living Jews in all of Nazi-dominated Europe. Had he been able to convince the Germans to delay the final deportation of the ghetto population that summer, or had the Russian Army, then encamped a short distance from the city's eastern edge, decided to advance sooner into Lodz, there is considerable speculation over the way Rumkowski's unflattering place in history would be seen today.)

Throne of Straw presents a wide spectrum of responses to Nazi persecution, as one character after another acts upon his or her understanding of the requirements for survival. Rumkowski's enforcer, Rabinowitz, the head of the Jewish police, betrays and humiliates other Jews. A young artist, Gabriel, anxious for preferment, does the same. His mother, Ada, offers sexual favors to Rumkowski in order to keep her family not just alive but together. Her father, Israel, gives up his pass to freedom for the sake of an orphan boy. One character goes crazy, several others join the partisans in the surrounding forests. In their ghetto environment, reduced to the most basic needs, some act selflessly, some selfishly. Yet we still try to distinguish among the victims by their final moments of *choice,* by their last ethical gesture before joining the dust of their ancestors. The Liebermans create their dramatic action from the idea that choice was possible; their Jewish characters are united by their desperate, albeit unsuccessful, struggle to survive.

Actually, there is one survivor in the play, the half-mad Hasid, Yankele, who narrates to the audience the conclusion of Rumkowski's story:

You're curious
I see it in your faces
You want to know what happened to him?
Well, as always with us, there are two possibilities.
A certain Mr. Levy swears he saw Rumkowski
Alongside the Commandant at Auschwitz
Reviewing the long lines of new arrivals and then taking his
place at the end of the line.
  However a kapo who worked the gas chambers
And wants his name withheld
Says that he was pushed in first
And that the reason he's so certain
Is that Miriam [Rumkowski's wife] was smiling, and that was highly unusual.
When the Russians finally arrived in Lodz
There were 801 Jews left. I am the one.
And why am I still here?
Because you are all still here.

(scene 12)

The Liebermans want to tell us about the Jews of Lodz because through them they are able to raise certain ethical questions that continually and universally trouble us, questions about the nature of good and evil, the complexity of motive, the meaning of responsibility, the possibility of faith, the fragility of moral assumption. But they also want to provide for audiences an image of survivorship that will unsettle and provoke. One clear conclusion of *Throne* is historically verifiable: that for almost all Jews in Lodz, regardless of religious, political, or social affinity, *nothing* availed. No choice, whether self-serving or altruistic, made any difference for survival. True, some lived longer than others and, for a while, better than others, but the results of their struggle led to an intractable, terminal sameness.

The one actual survivor is a homeless, destitute lunatic, obsessed with a mission to carry a message, not of truth but of skepticism, to his hearers. He concludes the play with a ready rebuke: to refrain from judging Rumkowski and the murdered millions until their lives are known and their conditions explained; only then can we resist facile moral assumptions which come from ignorance, hindsight, or condescension. In fact, the Liebermans reserve their judgment neither for Yankele nor Rumkowski. Instead they judge *us,* mostly casual survivors by accident of history or geography, whose privileged place too easily leads to historical misperception and self-serving betrayal of the victims of nazism.

The actions of the characters in *Throne* span the full range of responses to Nazi oppression because the Liebermans see all of them as possible for the Jews of the Holocaust, at least while the ghettos operated. The playwrights conceive of a large cast of characters whose behavior, taken together, reveals their understanding of the options for ethical action taken in extreme situations when survival is at stake. All the Jewish characters in their play, according to their own moral compass, try to locate the answer to the question: what price is acceptable to pay to survive? Some find an answer more easily than others. Those who are tested most cruelly are the characters (Ada, Israel, and Rumkowski's wife, Miriam) upon whom others rely for survival, which is why Rumkowski, upon whom *all* rely, embodies the most compelling, outrageous, and ambiguous dilemma. Interestingly, in *Throne of Straw,* we never learn *how* Yankele survived, his mordant wit notwithstanding (see chapter 3), while the others perished. But perhaps there is irony in that omission, or an uncomfortable truth—accidents also produced survivors. Still, Yankele's madness is as certain as his burden of witness, and helps to form the image of the actual survivor in our post-Holocaust world: skeptical, questioning, angry, isolated, despairing. The Liebermans' charge to us, who they see as survivors in a new twentieth-century sense, is a warning against easy moralizing and a plea to respect the actual survivor whose presence causes in us great confusion, embarrassment, and even resentment.

Shimon Wincelberg's *Resort 76* also uses the Lodz Ghetto as a setting for his Holocaust play, and his large cast of characters also confronts many moments where an action must be taken to assist in survival. Both *Resort 76* and *Throne of Straw* exploit the ghetto environment to allow for the existence of life-enhancing options. Both plays assume that, on the road to destruction, the ghetto became a place where autonomy was to a degree still possible. It is a distinction other writers often use and, as noted earlier, is part of the critical response to Bettelheim's stature and philosophy.

There are several overlapping stories told in *Resort 76*. The central figure is an engineer named Blaustain upon whose shoulders lies the triple burden of organizing the other workers in the ghetto factory, providing moral leadership to the group, and keeping himself alive and ethically responsible. He is filled with doubts about the sense and meaning of the tasks he undertakes and the usefulness of the actions he performs. Should he agree to the birth of his own child, considering his wife's sickly condition, the grim (or perhaps nonexistant) future awaiting the infant, and the danger the baby would cause for the others? Should he keep and protect the stray cat that has been entrusted to him by a neighbor, when he could trade it, or kill it and eat it for immediate benefit? Should he help the partisans in the forests outside the city and endanger his dependent, disputatious community? The other ghetto residents urge on him choices that confound his struggling moral nature.

Among the other characters in the play are Schnur, a teacher, and Beryl, his only pupil, who risk their lives to keep a semblance of Jewish tradition from being forgotten. They seek meaningful survival in intellectual and spiritual endeavor. Anya, Blaustain's sister, is a resistance fighter who determines that her survival depends on actively confronting the Germans. She rejects his "passive submission" in favor of armed struggle, seeking in violent confrontation a more honorable alternative to a life lived in subjugation and despair. Other characters desperately try to maintain some semblance of human dignity, including a German named Krause who has been mistakenly deported to the ghetto and who kills himself because he cannot face the shame he will encounter when his release is finally obtained.

At the play's end, the child will be born, the teacher will teach (although he is taken away to be shot), and the cat is turned loose. Even the animal, we are meant to understand, has a life that must not be taken needlessly, and although it is freer than the trapped, suffering people it leaves behind, its life of animal instinct is made clearly analogous to the oppressors of the ghetto population. On the other hand, the Jews' lives are enhanced and ennobled through the exercise of a moral choice. Although survival, for these characters, is nearly impossible, Wincelberg (whose play was inspired by Rachmil Bryks's short story "A Cat in the Ghetto") leaves little doubt as to his preferences for making sense of survival, which is why he purposefully concludes the play *before* most of his characters are destroyed. For this reason, *Resort 76* is among the most optimistic of Holocaust dramas and, to those who insist that note must be taken of the nearly total extermination of Lodz's Jews, largely untrue.

Both George Tabori's *The Cannibals* and Charlotte Delbo's *Who Will Carry the Word?* are set inside concentration camps, where, as noted earlier, testimony often tells us there was no opportunity to exercise choice, at least choice in the traditional sense, or with its usual meaning. Tabori's play raises the issue of whether it is morally correct to commit any act to survive, in this case cannibalism. The dozen men in the cast of characters are all, except for two actual survivors, the sons of the Nazis' victims, i.e., they are "playing" their dead fathers. In reenacting their fathers' lives, they are ordered by the SS guard, called the Angel of Death, to eat bits of the body of their dead comrade in order to survive at least a little while longer. All but two refuse, and all but those two are killed. In order to survive they must commit an abhorrent act, and in performing it deny the existence of that which is most essentially "human." By consuming Puffi's flesh, the survivors, Hirschler and Heltai, represent one idea: that surviving is worthwhile at *any* cost. Even degraded life has value, they assert, when the alternative is a quick death in the name of ideals that are worth defending only in a social world where humane deeds fit a defined and operative ethical structure. Clearly no such order was to be found in Auschwitz. In fact, the surrealism of *The Cannibals* is part of an artistic attempt to reveal theatrically the moral chaos, brutality, and madness of the concentrationary universe.

In addition, the language of *The Cannibals* rises to a hysterical eloquence in its repudiation of God. This theme is one of the central concerns of Holocaust writing that advances the belief that to accept a God who is just and humane is impossible after the Holocaust. Survival is shown to depend on human, not divine, action. The murder of one-third of the world's Jews, many writers argue, is sufficient proof of divine indifference or abandonment and signifies the end of the four thousand-year-old covenant with Abraham. Nonetheless, Heltai and Hirschler act to insure their survival, but they are unsympathetically presented, their lives seem cheap and shallow, and they are, above all, cannibals, for whom positive feelings are nearly impossible to hold. Tabori appears to respond favorably to the decision of the doomed men who chose not to eat human flesh, while he disapproves of those who did. Yet, such a simple judgment is inadequate, especially in light of the fact that the survival of the two "cannibals" has enabled the story of *all* the prisoners to be "told." Thus, even in granting a moment of choice for his play's victims, Tabori creates an environment barren of hope and devoid of any concrete answer to the question of how or whether meaningful survival can be achieved.

Who Will Carry the Word? also takes place inside a concentration camp, presumably Auschwitz, where its author, Charlotte Delbo, spent many months. The play is distinguished by its poetic language, its large, entirely female cast, and its contribution to Holocaust drama of the experience of death and survival of the non-Jews who suffered under the Nazis. The play begins with twenty-two women who arrive together as political deportees, and concludes with only two of the women left alive. In the penultimate scene, one of the group has just killed herself on the electrified wire rather than participate in the "White Kerchief Kommando," the group of inmates who prepared the arriving children for their death. As in *The Cannibals,* Delbo seems to validate the final choice reserved to concentrate camp prisoners, that of suicide. By that action, Gina refuses to give assent to the inhumanity of her enemies, despite the recognition that it will have no effect on the agenda of death the Nazis are committed to carrying out. In fact, it may have a negative effect of diminishing the resistance of the remaining women by increasing their despair. Françoise, one of the final two survivors, recapitulates her camp experience to the audience, recalling (in details congenial to Des Pres's assumptions) both the physical pain and the comradely sustenance that characterized her ordeal.

> We have seen, side by side, the worst cruelty and the greatest beauty. I mean those who practically carried me in their arms when I couldn't walk, those who gave me their tea when I was choking from thirst when my tongue was like a piece of rough wood in my mouth, those who touched my hand and managed to

form a smile on their chapped lips when I was desperate, those who picked me up when I fell in the mud when they were so weak themselves, those who took my feet in their hands at night when we were going to sleep, and who blew on them when I felt they had begun to freeze. And here I am. They all died for me. No one dies for anyone else in life.

(act 3, scene 3)

Françoise's greatest anguish, however, results from her concern for her future as a survivor, from her fear that articulating her Holocaust story will cause others to reject not only herself but also the whole experience of the death camps as being too improbable and horrifying to be believed. Her future, if she does survive, will be one of rejection and alienation, and her mission to testify on behalf of those who perished (to "carry the word") will involve an additional suffering that comes with the betrayal of the victims by an uncomprehending, unsympathetic public.

Delbo's play is noteworthy for its visual and linguistic images of women, for gender plays a crucial role in the power of the play. The women in *Who Will Carry the Word?* function as a group, living and dying while maintaining an attitude of mutual support. In assisting each other through acts of bravery or the imagination, they demonstrate a deep quality of sharing and a profound sense of the human connection unseen in most other Holocaust plays. Faced with unrelenting suffering and certain death, they represent images of humane, noncompetitive cooperation in the most extreme situations, while *at the same time* emphasizing to us how useless to survival that behavior was. Because Delbo is interested in the experience of these women, an experience expressed in interrogative as well as poetic terms, *Who Will Carry the Word?* depicts the artist's search to make sense of the choices that resulted in the deaths of the victims as well as the lives of the survivors.

IV

I have argued that the notion of survival, "survivorship," is a concept that artists may engage for a variety of reasons. Taken together, however, the images of survival provide no clear conclusion concerning what choices we should make or lessons we should draw about our future as individuals, peoples, or nations in our continuing confrontation with genocidal violence and universal suffering. Indisputably, the power of images of goodness is satisfying and perhaps even necessary to our survival; but the truth of those images, theatrical and otherwise, is by no means universally or clearly established. Similar conclusions may be reached concerning our responses to images of evil. As Lawrence Langer has shrewdly observed: "Virtually every statement about the death camps contains the seeds of its own contradiction. . . ."[27]

The complexity of the artist's obligation to Holocaust material begins from the moment that material is engaged. By imagining characters who are survivors, depicting their experience, and assessing their behavior, playwrights create images of continuance that are informed by their own biases as well as by modern history. They inevitably raise ethical questions about how survival was achieved, how it can be maintained, how it can be *used* as a guide for the future; nonetheless, no single answer exists, only irony, ambiguity, and paradox. David Roskies, in *Against the Apocalypse,* writes about his own work:

> My book that on the surface deals with finality, endings, disruption, and desecration is really a study in continuities and internal transformations. Jewish catastrophe is a subject whose paradoxical nature—life in death—challenges some of our basic assumptions.[28]

To readers of Holocaust literature and audiences of Holocaust theatre, that conclusion is neither new or sufficient, but it represents a starting point for a search that can have no satisfactory end but must be undertaken nonetheless. The images of survival we confront in Holocaust drama ultimately influence and are influenced by what we believe about the issue at the heart of the Holocaust experience: the nature and possibility of choice. That subject, and the hope it arouses or defeats in us, is the lasting and continuing focus of the theatre of the Holocaust, and the inquiry that will shed light on the darkness we all carry.

Two

Tragedy and the Holocaust

And yet, first of all, I should like to slaughter one or two men, just to throw off the concentration camp mentality, the effects of continual subservience, the effects of helplessly watching others being beaten and murdered, the effects of all this horror. I suspect, though, that I will be marked for life. I do not know whether we shall survive, but I like to think that one day we shall have the courage to tell the world the whole truth and call it by its proper name.

—Tadeusz Borowski
"Auschwitz, Our Home (A Letter)"

I

Aʀᴛɪsᴛs and their critics live with the hard and humbling truth that their writing keeps raising the same questions that have been asked for centuries. They also live with the harder truth that despite passion and concern, the answers to significant moral and aesthetic questions remain elusive. What *has* changed over the course of much time, especially the accelerated time of the last half-century, is the awareness of a greater urgency to these questions and a greater burden we carry to them. The issue of tragedy, of its nature and possibility, and of how it is related to the Holocaust is the two-edged problem I would like to discuss.

In the considerable debate over the relationship of Holocaust literature to tragedy, much attention has focused on the characteristics that distinguish tragedy from other theatrical forms, i.e., comedy and tragicomedy. But before that problem can be addressed, it is necessary to decide where to search for the characteristics that contribute to what can be called tragic in drama: in the play's elements ("the tragic character" or "the tragic action"), in the audience ("the tragic response"), or in the playwright ("the tragic vision"). Since Aristotle, these have been the places where the confirmation of the tragic experience can be found.

The kinds of plays that comprise the theatre of the Holocaust usually describe the lives of Jews who succumbed to or survived Nazi persecution. Their stories have both a historical and a fictional dimension. That these victims of violence possess distinguishing characteristics—of their conditions or of their actions—that permit them to represent us, or at least most of us, seems to me indisputable. And because all serious drama seeks its effects through identification with stage characters and emblematic settings, it is possible that the Jewish character in the Holocaust context may represent all people, Jew and non-Jew, in the description of universal human conditions.

There is, of course, much debate over whether tragedy can be written at all in the twentieth century, and the dramatized Holocaust experience that reaches for the tragic condition adds to the debate. At various times over the last several generations, the impossibility of writing tragedy has been credited to a host of disparate (often contradictory) causes, including nineteenth-century theories of determinism, Freudian psychology, political democracy, rejection of classical artistic forms, twentieth-century theories of existential meaninglessness, and Christian salvation. Yet tragedy, or at least the *idea* of tragedy, refuses to die despite the eloquent refutations of numerous critics, among whom George Steiner is one.

Steiner, a prolific and wide-ranging commentator on culture in general and European literatures in particular, has written with extraordinary insight into the issues raised by the Holocaust and its literary manifestations. He was among the earliest critics whose expansive preoccupations with the Holocaust included an anxious personal statement for the future of the Jewish people combined with a professional concern for the implications of genocide on dramatic form. Among Steiner's earliest important works was *The Death of Tragedy* (1961), a book that surveys the history of Western literature with the objective of charting the demise of the tragic possibility in literary creation. Curiously, *The Death of Tragedy* begins with a brief discussion of the relationship between "the Judaic sense of the world" and tragedy, a relationship Steiner describes as one of alienation, but one he rarely attends to again in the course of his book. He writes: "The Judaic spirit is vehement in its conviction that the order of the universe and of man's estate is accessible to reason."[1]

Steiner believes that tragedy can flourish only alongside a conviction of the world's essential irrationality, a perspective on life that was unavailable to the Jews from their earliest days as a people because of the rational bias of their culture. He argues that as Western society became increasingly drawn to the rational, a shift that culminated in the nineteenth century and the Age of Reason, Western art became less tragic. At the conclusion of his book, he implies that tragedy becomes possible again when cultures become *less* rational in behavior and belief. In a later essay, "A Kind of Survivor" (1964), Steiner surveys the eternal status of Jews as the scapegoat of the world's other religions and calls this permanent condition of persecution "a condition almost beyond rational understanding."[2] Acknowledging his Jewishness, he is able to describe himself as "a kind of survivor" despite his geographical distance from the Holocaust in Europe.

By accepting the historical, *inevitable* fact of the Jews' persecution across centuries, and by focusing his attention on the irrational terminus of irrational behavior, the Holocaust, Steiner edges closer to relocating the true tragic material for contemporary literary and dramatic expression in the murder of six million Jews between 1939 and 1945. In the *failure* of rationality in the enlightened center of Europe, he comes to see the crucial, paradoxical event of modern times.

> Why did humanistic traditions and models of conduct prove so fragile a barrier against political bestiality? In fact, were they a barrier, or is it more realistic to perceive in humanistic culture express solicitations of authoritarian rule and cruelty?[3]

At the same time that Steiner discovers terror, confusion, and identity, he also discovers in the Holocaust a countervailing positive force that produces a restored aesthetic opportunity; tragedy, purchased at the price of one-third of his people, may be a kind of perverse reward of their destruction. This conclusion poses the possibility of reawakened tragedy and a reawakening cultural heritage as the result of an abominable historical event. (I sense that this recognition created serious psychological discomfort for Steiner, which can be seen in his response to the criticism of his 1982 novella *The Portage to San Cristobal of A.H.* and the play adapted from it by Christopher Hampton the following year. I discuss the play and its reception in chapter 4.)

Steiner thus locates in his heritage and in recent history the material that can produce, in the right hands, the tragic vision. Based on a millennial vocation for suffering that, arriving at the Holocaust, continues to elude understanding despite the most thorough of cultural investigations, Steiner's personal journey seems to have returned him to the tragic mystery after a lifelong search. While struggling to make sense of the most irrational event in modern history, applying a deeply rational energy to it, he finds only warning, frustration, and fear. Yet, if traditional tragedy flourished in an ancient world characterized by ignorance, faith, turbulence, suffering, and death, then the Holocaust, from the perspective of artists and critics, replicates those same conditions, enabling (if it were desired) the rediscovery of the idea of the tragic. Simply, in the record of humiliations endured through time and across continents, in the mad hatred against Jews, may be found the organizing experience of tragedy.

Drawing himself back into the history of his people, Steiner has given a new legitimacy and a new context to his historical-aesthetic investigations. At the same time, he appears to admit the failure of his search to produce results that are fully understandable, not to say consoling. In Richmond Hathorn's terms, he has perceived in his life both objective dilemmas and subjective confusions, turning to criticism and then to art to relax the grip of his discomfort. In Jewish myth and history he has found material endlessly provocative and mysterious which pressures him to "acknowledge that the existence of . . . ignorance is itself inevitable."[4] The conclusion also seems inevitable: the dramatizing of the irrational loss of human life in an unfathomable universe, which began in ancient Greece, continues in the work of contemporary playwrights challenged by the Holocaust's conditions of suffering and mystery.

There is, as has been pointed out by commentators on the Holocaust, a double danger in rediscovering one's heritage in the attempted destruction of it.[5] First, of lesser interest, is that the rediscovery may result in living negatively, i.e., of wanting to frustrate your enemies as a way to maintain your own continuance. Of greater importance is that it can blind the individual to the positive, life-affirming, and beautiful aspects of one's culture and history. In the context of the Holocaust, this second problem can be minimized by playwrights who, while acknowledging the magnitude of the destruction, revert to the older, traditional artistic forms to convey a more positive design and significance in the world. Further, if Steiner's long struggle can be seen as a model critical and personal journey, his assertion of a renewed tragic possibility in effect neutralizes the following specific objections of three critics who maintain that Holocaust material is unavailable for tragic theatrical presentation:

1. Stephen Spender's assessment, derived from his study of Holocaust poetry, that "the anonymous victim is, in the Western tradition, no subject for tragedy;"[6]

2. Terrence Des Pres's belief, derived from his important study of life in concentration camps, that the "tragic hero finds in death a victory. . . . He is proof of spirit's contempt for the flesh, and death itself becomes a confirmation of the greatness. There is much to be admired in such a stance, but not in the time of plague;"[7]

3. Lawrence Langer's assertion that "man's fate in the death camps can never be 'celebrated' through the traditional forms of tragic experience."[8]

In the face of the intractable demands of dramatic presentation, including the need to identify emotionally with characters portrayed on stage as dynamic individuals by live performers, Holocaust material confronts playwrights with a situation that appears to *restrict* the creation of tragic images and experiences in at least four ways: the anonymity of the victims' death (untragic characters), the seeming meaninglessness of their suffering (untragic vision), the circumscribed nature of the actions available to the protagonists (untragic action), and the unavailability of certain emotional options to the audience (untragic response). Can playwrights overcome these obstacles and provide moving and meaningful portrayals of characters caught acting in their destructive history?

Playwrights who respond affirmatively are likely to believe that traditional tragedy provides an appropriate form for the story they have to tell. Some have continued to fashion characters and plays faithful to classical tragic models (of which *Oedipus the King* is one paradigm) by describing protagonists whose heroic stature is confirmed by their choosing actions that are then shown to determine their fate. In other words, some playwrights continue to create characters who possess the individual autonomy to influence their future and who behave in ways that affirm universal values amid their personal and terminal distress. The clearest examples (but not the only ones) of this type of character are found in plays written about historical figures: Janusz Korczak, Hannah Senesh, or Anne Frank—characters who defy group identity and anonymous death and who contradict the restrictive conditions of helplessness and futility to achieve a personal triumph that accompanies their destruction.[9]

Understandably, the sharpest refutation of the "sense" of these plays is historical and cultural in nature. First, the totality of the Holocaust overwhelms (or negates) the small, occasional examples of resistance or integrity. Second, the larger artistic problem of postwar writing, which Wylie Sypher has called the "loss of the self," also impinges on the tragic form by locating, in a more general sense, the diminishment of the human figure by technology. Sypher writes:

> We have already reached the crux of our problem: Is it possible, while the individual is vanishing behind the functionary throughout the technological world, to have any sort of humanism that does not depend on the older notions of the self, the independent self that is outdated or at least victimized by the operations of power on its present scale? Any such humanism must come to terms with our sense of anonymity of the self, must therefore get beyond any romantic notion of selfhood.[10]

In the light of the historical concreteness of Hitler's "final solution to the Jewish question" (a product of the Nazis' technical mastery) and the cultural decline of the autonomous citizen, it can be argued that humanity is literally *and* metaphorically shrunken, making any positive image less tenable and harder to accept in the modern world. Anonymity seems to attach itself to life *and* death in the Holocaust. In addition, because of "the privileged position of the Holocaust reader" as " 'collaborative' " witness to the events recounted,[11] the loss of self involves a moral as well as a historical and cultural dimension.[12]

Nonetheless, if a belief in the efficacy of traditional forms can be sustained, or a fear of anonymous, meaningless life and death rejected (*which amounts to the same thing*), it is possible that "positive" plays about the Holocaust can be accepted on their own terms and judged for their honesty and effectiveness. Above all, the need these plays fill in the lives of audiences and playwrights must be acknowledged.

> . . . an essential part of our conviction that an experience [in the theatre] is momentous derives from what we take to be the import of the play.
> . . . if part of this conviction derives from what the play means, another part derives from the mere fact *that* it means. Meaningfulness is itself momentous for human beings, as they discover, *a contrario,* whenever life has no meaning for them. All art serves as a

lifeboat to rescue us from the ocean of meaninglessness—an extraordinary service to perform at any time and more than ever when
religion and philosophy prove less and less able to perform it. To
be thus rescued is to rediscover our personal dignity, through
which alone we can discover dignity in others, dignity in human
life as such.[13]

This traditional belief in art and its ethical function cannot attract
all artists, but it has exercised a considerable influence on a number of
playwrights who have taken up the Holocaust theme. Their objective is
more than the creation of a "momentary stay against confusion" (in
Robert Frost's phrase), but it certainly encompasses that. It involves a
formal program or strategy for dealing with the terror and mystery of
human experience in a Holocaust or post-Holocaust world. Taken to
an unwholesome extreme, these plays may define a sentimental or
delusionary picture of the world devoid of any sense of historical
catastrophe, as Lawrence Langer has pointed out.[14] But, when playwrights sincerely adhere to this belief as a genuine aesthetic (and thus
moral) option, audiences witness images of a world whose values can
confront meaningless, terrible existence with the implication that, in
special cases at least, victory is in some small way possible. And, according to traditional tragedy, the individuals who do challenge the
forces of catastrophic fate *are* unique, like us and different from us at
the same time. Whether or not this strategy is irresponsible and childish
or necessary and courageous, we do not seem wholly able to dispense
with the hopeful and heroic aspects of tragedy. And although sorely
tempted, neither can most artists *totally* sacrifice their intuitive,
natural use of some life-affirming action, even in the presence of concentration camps. Robert J. Lifton identifies this condition, which
helps to explain (but for some, not excuse) the reluctance to jettison
traditional dramatic forms:

> A Western world would [fail] if it sought to cope with a massive
> death immersion by totally abandoning the emotional and lit-
> erary heritage of tragedy. While tragedy posits a heroic struggle
> against death-linked destiny. . . , [it is] a means of reasserting
> a connection, integrity, and movement necessary for symbolic
> integrity . . .[15]

II

As a theatrical character, the figure of Janusz Korczak has come to
represent the qualities of integrity, responsibility, and courage that

enhance the image of the Holocaust's victims, who so often are pictured as compromising, passive, and helpless. In his decision to shield the children in his care from the worst horrors of their deportation—and in his determination to adhere to a philosophy of respect, responsibility, and love for people of all ages despite penalty of terrible death—he has been embraced by numerous playwrights as a forceful, positive counterweight to the denial of meaning and the anonymity of death so often stressed in the recounting of the Holocaust experience. In the same historical experience where others find nihilism and unredeemed suffering, these playwrights (with varying degrees of success and assurance) discover evidence of heroism and humane possibility. All retain the sense of extraordinary loss (seen in the deaths of Korczak and the children he cared for), but they refuse to relinquish the positive image without which their vision of the moral world would totally collapse. Thus, they reject outright the notion of circumscribing human action to the degree that it denies the tragic vision, as Walter Kerr has shown:

> There is only one development chilling enough to have done the job [of killing off tragedy]. Man would have had to press beyond the business of analyzing his freedom to act, beyond watching himself in a mirror as he debated whether or not he might responsibly use his freedom to act. He would have had to come to disbelieve in his freedom to act. He would have had to deny freedom itself in order to kill tragedy.[16]

Erwin Sylvanus's play *Dr. Korczak and the Children* (see chapter 5) is perhaps the best-known play on the life of Korczak, winning the Leo Baeck Prize in 1958; more recent plays by Tamara Karren (*Who Was That Man?*) and Gabriel Emanuel (*Children of the Night*) are not as dramatically skilled. But of all the Korczak plays, it is Michael Brady's *Korczak's Children* that deserves more attention than it has received, for it possesses considerable theatrical power and can shed much light on the possibilities for one kind of a tragic retelling of the Holocaust experience.[17]

Korczak's Children focuses on Korczak's efforts to save his orphanage and provide for its children, but Brady broadens the action to include a fuller discussion of the historical and cultural context in which Korczak lived and worked. The play begins with the orphanage children performing a little play about Poland's King Casimir, who, despite counsel to the contrary, is determined to protect Poland's Jewish population. Outside in the Warsaw street, a Polish mob is threatening them all with violence; inside, the children are starving.

There is both charm and irony in this little playlet for, in 1942, there was no one to protect the Jews, and their condition was truly desperate. For the rest of the play, Korczak, with little success and diminishing hope, will attempt to extract from potential benefactors some assistance for the children in his care.

A secondary figure in the play is Emmanuel Ringelblum. Ringelblum was the noted historian of the Warsaw Ghetto, whose determination to collect the written materials of its daily life helped to preserve for later generations the primary evidence of awful existence. Here, Ringelblum has tutored the same three children who acted in the "King Casimir" story to learn enough about the Catholic religion so they might pass as non-Jews outside the ghetto walls. On "the other side," they can smuggle food or weapons, kill German soldiers, or, if the ghetto is liquidated, escape into the surrounding Polish territory and fight for their survival. "You called them your magnificent children," says Ringelblum to Korczak,

> I agree. You've taught them loyalty, belief in an ideal world, sacrifice for the good of the group. If the Gestapo close off this street and I have twenty minutes to pull Hanna and Moski and Mendel into the sewer, will they come if they see the orphanage about to be evacuated? You must cut the cord, Janusz.
>
> (act 1, scene 1)

In the play, it is important that Korczak and Ringelblum are *not* enemies, although they do confront their terrible dilemma with differing responses. Still, they clearly respect each other, and Korczak orders the three children to prepare for evacuating the orphanage in accordance with the training that Ringelblum has provided for them.

In succeeding scenes, Korczak is tormented by the Nazis and, at the conclusion of act 1, asks advice of his assistant Stefania Wilczynska: should he begin instructing the children in Jewish heritage and prayer? He has resisted this sort of indoctrination in the belief that young people must not be coerced in matters of religion. But, in desperation, it is clear that Korczak realizes that something spiritual is absent in his much-abused life, and that his starving children also need more sustenance than they are receiving. Reduced to tears, Korczak, wearing a prayer shawl, expresses his frustration and despair in a "talk with God."

In act 2, the deportation order is conveyed by a young German soldier who, many years before the war, had himself been cared for in Korczak's orphanage. Later, the scene shifts to a dream sequence in the country a week before the outbreak of the war; we see the children and their elders enjoying a picnic on church land, whose use they have humbly requested. The little vacation is intended, Ringelblum and Korczak recognize, as "a Chekhovian moment of peacefulness" before the breaking storm. (Chekhov is Korczak's favorite author.) In the "dream," the children march "to the sun" and escape, but in reality (as prefigured earlier in the boy Hirsz's dream) death awaits them all. The final words we hear are the voice of a "neutral" narrator describing the destruction of the ghetto and the heroic finish to Korczak's life. The concluding image is of Korczak, alone onstage, crushing the suicide pills he had kept for himself, and making his single statement: "If my presence will save even one child one second of terror, my life will be well lost."

It is Brady's intention to present a tragic Korczak, founder of his own "Children's Republic," doomed to death by his Nazi antagonists. He attempts no "message" for us, but instead offers a perspective on the Holocaust that, because of its particular positive imagery, conveys a sense of renewal and possibility. This is especially true because the burden of the loss falls on the small shoulders of the children, all of whom perished, but whose lives are preserved in the continual retelling of Korczak's story. (The play's title refers to them, but the play's action, moral and physical, centers on Korczak.) Instilled with Korczak's humane teaching about the respect and love due them and all people, they carry a legacy of hope despite the terrible fate that befell them. For Brady, it seems, the mystery of goodness is even greater than the mystery of evil, and it is with the former that his sympathies clearly lie.

The enormous question of why the Nazis murdered six million Jews (including one and a half million children) will certainly continue for the foreseeable future, and historians and others will emphasize economic, historical, political, cultural, and psychological or other reasons for the "final solution." But, remembering Steiner, the strongest argument for maintaining the sense of tragic mystery is that *no rational investigation* completely explains the Holocaust—not the fears and beliefs of the obsessed German leadership, not the dislocations following the First World War, not the vague but powerful psychological and cultural needs of an acquiescing population, not the agony of the Nazis' victims. In these plays, the heroic figure assumes a tragic stature that, *validated by history,* guides the audience's attention to images of moral repair in a violent world that is out of ethical control. Thus, while the Holocaust as an all-encompassing historical event remains in large degree intellectually impenetrable, in its smaller aspects or details playwrights discern a meaningful rescue of humane possibility. From an aesthetic point of view the danger to this strategy is the same as in any tragic writing: making too explicit or too easy the restoration of a moral order. "How much darkness must we acknowledge before we will be able to confess that the Holocaust story cannot be told in terms of heroic dignity, moral courage, and the triumph of the human spirit in adversity?" asks Lawrence Langer.[18] No answer is possible or necessary for playwrights who reject the question, refusing to be separated from a traditional tragic perspective. Taking refuge in those older forms, they aim to succeed in the kind of aesthetic—and moral—victory described by Richard Sewell:

> There has been suffering and disaster, ultimate and irredeemable loss, and there is a promise of more to come. But all who have been involved have been witness to new revelations about human existence, the evil of evil and the goodness of good. They are more "ready." The same old paradoxes and ambiguities remain, but for the moment they are transcended in the higher vision.[19]

III

But by highlighting the heroism of Korczak or Hannah Senesh or Anne Frank, playwrights may be seen as departing from traditional tragic form in another way: by eliminating the protagonist's culpability in his or her own destruction. An impetuous Senesh (the young Jew who parachuted behind Nazi lines and was captured and executed in 1944) or an occasionally intemperate Korczak are only feeble attempts to "humanize" them and show a flaw in an otherwise perfect character. In part this is because, in searching the Holocaust for dramatic material, the impermissible premise is the one that asserts that Jews brought their destruction on themselves. Thus, the aspect of a protagonist's guilt traditionally associated with the tragic form is exceedingly difficult to sustain.

In responding to this aesthetic problem, playwrights have resorted to two additional but differing approaches that allow for continued adherence to moral images and tragic form concerning the creation of stage characters.

1. They have subsumed the individual figures into a larger portrait where differences among characters are rejected in favor of the universality of the group protagonist.

2. They have provided around the protagonist a range of characters who reveal different and often contradictory responses to oppression, so that some individual Jews *do* contribute to the mechanism of death that has trapped them.

Each of these approaches requires a philosophical decision concerning where to locate the source of evil in human beings. The first strategy stresses the human capacity for goodness and sees evil "out there," that is, in a contaminated, threatening world determined to destroy any evidence of righteousness. The second strategy locates the source of evil *in* people, and finds in human weakness permission to settle upon the Holocaust's victims an otherwise unavailable tragic guiltiness. (This condition is validated less by history and more by an understanding of human psychology that sees people behaving naturally in their own self-interest in times of great personal threat.)

The classical tragic model for the first type of play is *The Trojan Women*. Euripides, in his play about the destruction of a city and a whole people, gathers his suffering multitudes for a final, if futile, spasm of resistance to genocide. *The Trojan Women*, in fact, is even bleaker in outlook than most tragedies, classical or modern, because it concludes with the destruction of the last male in Troy, the boy Astyanax. The Greeks throw him from the city's walls, and his death signals the end of a proud and great nation; at the play's conclusion, the abused women survivors are led away to be the spoils of war for their enemies.

The lament of *The Trojan Women*, joined into a single voice of suffering, embodies a powerful condemnation of war and those who carry out war. For our purposes, it becomes important as a tragic model for modern playwrights who treat the Holocaust theme and who seek to stress the monumentality of the terror in the last moments of victims who were, and who remain, essentially innocent. In a way, these playwrights make a virtue out of anonymity. The twenty-two women prisoners who are incarcerated in Auschwitz at the beginning of Charlotte Delbo's *Who Will Carry The Word?* are in a situation similar to their Trojan ancestors. Slowly decreased by murder and suicide in the course of Delbo's play, their situation is postexilic, that is, after the deportation. In the closing moments, only two women remain alive to direct at the audience (and by implication all people who have not suffered as they have) the "word" they are charged with carrying. They speak, but with Cassandra-like misgivings. They fear that the concentration camp experiences are too gruesome and appalling to be believed. "Why should you believe those stories of ghosts," asks Françoise, "ghosts who came back and who are not able to explain how?"[20]

Delbo's interest is in the fate of non-Jewish political victims of the Nazis, but her theme concerns how small groups of survivors affect the mass of uncaring, uncomprehending, larger groups of postwar citizens. It is a problem that continues to confront all survivors as the Holocaust moves further from us in time. Delbo's skill in presenting the group's story accumulates power as it shows their numbers decreasing. She asserts the qualities of innocence, courage, and compassionate cooperation, the last quality appearing here and elsewhere in Holocaust drama as especially feminine. She laments the destruction of those precious values to the point where succeeding generations—precisely because of this loss—cannot believe, let alone accept, the reality of history.

Liliane Atlan, in *Monsieur Fugue or Earth Sick,* also stresses the innocence and purity lost to the world at the hands of the Nazis.[21] Among the factors influencing the writing of the play is the Korczak story, to which Atlan directly refers in an epigraph appended to the printed text. The play itself describes the last journey of a group of four children, "almost animals if it were not for their mad eyes," who have survived in the sewers "after the total destruction of a ghetto." The play begins and ends with an image of fire, first of the ghetto burning in the distance, and later at the edge of the pit used to incinerate the corpses of the Nazis' victims.

Accompanied by an innocent German soldier, Grol (also known as Monsieur Fugue), a "sweet and simple [and] very disturbing" deserter from the Nazi ideology of death, the four children ride to their destruction through a fog-filled night (*"nacht und nebel"*) on the back of a truck. The action mostly consists of the children's fantasies of a different, although no happier, life, which are "acted out" by the five innocents. They assume the identities of various characters from their past and their imagined, foreclosed, future, and they play the roles of various animals and objects, one of which is a large doll that "carries" the soul of one of the deceased friends of the children. At the play's conclusion, under the supervision of their murderers, the children, who have become "very old," walk to their fiery death in "The Valley of Bones" (a biblical allusion that Sylvanus, in his Korczak play, used with less irony and greater optimism as a prophecy of resurrection).

Monsieur Fugue is a heartbreaking play, surreal in its conception and poetic in its language. Its evocative power comes from its relentless image of childhood defiled in the Nazi land of fog and flame. The innocence and purity of all children—qualities only occasionally seen here, since the four young people begin the play possessed by a frightening savagery—are what Atlan laments for. Her victims, including the childlike Monsieur Fugue, are memorable not as individuals (they often exchange identities) but as a group. Their death, like the Trojan boy's, is meant to represent the irreparable loss to all people whose very continuance as recognizably human creatures is rendered impossible by the deadly effects of Nazi ideology taken to its inevitable extreme. "That, that's not just," concludes Raissa about the world before she hobbles to her death. "That's dirt. I don't understand why God does dirt to children. I'm not good for anything anymore."

George Tabori, in *The Cannibals*,[22] adjusts the strategy for the group portrait only slightly, but with important ramifications. His play, as I described in the previous chapter, is set in a concentration camp barracks where a group of starving prisoners (not all Jewish) are forced to confront a hideous moral choice: accept their dead comrade's flesh as food and live, or reject cannibalism and be immediately killed. The "choice" is forced upon them by the Nazi "Angel of Death," SS Shreckinger, who makes his ultimatum only moments after the prisoners *as a group* have decided *not* to eat human flesh. Although we have watched the prisoners retell stories of previous moral lapses and criminal behavior, by finally rejecting the human meal—as all except two of the prisoners do—they seem to have regained some sort of positive image of human behavior despite their abominably degraded circumstances. The two "survivors," Heltai and Hirschler, serve as narrators of the grim story and appear as unhappy and lonely individuals; their comrades in the reenactment of the story are the surviving sons of their dead "fathers." Those who go to their deaths, now joined together by an extraordinary renewal of moral purpose, actually seem to regain some measure of recognizable humanity.

In rejecting cannibalism, the majority of Tabori's characters establish a bond between them which has the effect of restoring a kind of damaged innocence and irreducable humanity, the crucial characteristics of the group protagonist. Shreckinger torments them with the accusation that "there is a Fuehrer in the asshole of the best of us," but except for Heltai and Hirschler, the charge is disproved. As with Atlan's *Monsieur Fugue*, and to a lesser extent, with Delbo's *Who Will Carry the Word?*, an extraordinary, phantasmagorical setting seems to focus our attention on the human figure in its fragility and vulnerability while at the same time emotionally conveying the texture of the terrifying violence responsible for the destruction of individual identity. The individual is subsumed into a group protagonist who confronts an external evil and maintains (or reclaims) a stature of innocence by finding courage and a reflected dignity in the companionship of peers, a fidelity to goodness, and a yearning for freedom. The destruction of the group protagonist in the plays, either by attrition or by sudden, multiple termination, creates a moving image of suffering and resistance whereby anonymity is simultaneously created and transcended by desperate positive behavior, which, though unavailing to survival, validates for audiences a moral option available to *all* people even in the worst of times.

Resort 76, by Shimon Wincelberg,[23] in its description of a wide range of character and action, is the best example of a play that combines the two kinds of dramatic strategies discussed earlier. Unwilling to discard the image of a tragic hero, Wincelberg crowds around his protagonist Blaustain a group of characters who challenge his battered innocence, take advantage of his generosity, and distract him from his personal search for a moral basis for his own life. The play is strongest in its depiction of a variety of character types, less satisfying in the methods it uses to achieve a conclusion with a positive statement about ghetto life in the Holocaust. In fact, Wincelberg, in setting all the action of his play in the Lodz Ghetto *prior* to its destruction, mitigates somewhat the sense of catastrophe that pervades most Holocaust drama. His objective is to leave us with the strongest possible image of humane behavior under abominable circumstances.

Blaustain is faced with a series of moral dilemmas that require urgent resolution because of the time limits established in the story and because the other characters of the ghetto factory he heads demand his counsel in solving their problems. In a position of some responsibility, his trials are everybody's. As noted in chapter 1, in the course of the play, Blaustain must decide whether to give up his position and flee the ghetto for the forests to join the armed resistance; whether the child his pregnant wife is carrying should be born; whether to hide a cat entrusted to him by other ghetto residents.

Blaustain makes the "right," i.e., moral, decisions, affirming life on all counts. In the process, Wincelberg somewhat diminishes the sense of tragedy the play conveys because the pressure of death is alleviated through the continuance of the ghetto environment, and because of the obvious dependency on melodramatic (structural) artifice. At the same time, Wincelberg does acknowledge the presence of death, as Schnur, the teacher, is taken away by the Nazis, and Krause, the German "outsider" among them dies by his own hand. Nonetheless, *Resort 76* undermines the dramatic inevitability associated with the life of a tragic protagonist or group. With less at stake than Brady's Korczak, Wincelberg (a genuinely compassionate witness) guides his protagonist back into a group that, at the play's conclusion, is purged of moral confusions and ambiguities that baffle the more tragic protagonists of other Holocaust dramas whose dilemmas have no simple solutions.

The play's weakness is perhaps its partaking of the several formal options of this kind of Holocaust drama without clearly committing itself to one of them. In a final assessment, Wincelberg's group portrait of solidarity amid suffering is less demanding than that of Delbo's women or Atlan's children because it exchanges the pressures of imminent and complete destruction for a more deliberately positive picture of victims under something slightly less than maximum penalty. With the tragic context somewhat diminished, the kind of emotional effect *Resort 76* finally achieves is a worthy mixture of sadness and hopefulness, secured by human tenacity in the face of intermittent violence, and perhaps touched by an air of unreality when we remember the actual fate of the Lodz Ghetto.

The second type of tragic Holocaust drama is based on the playwright's acceptance of evil *inside* of all of us, even the Holocaust's victims. From the historical perspective, the assignment of mass ethical failure to the Jews is irrelevant and irresponsible, simply because there is little evidence for attributing the responsibility for the Jews' destruction to themselves. But from a theatrical perspective, this approach assumes crucial importance, for neglecting this aspect of negative human behavior would eliminate useful *dramatic* choices and, to a lesser extent, would reject the occasional evidence that *some* Jews, like so many others at that time in Europe, behaved badly. Here playwrights focus on the most volatile of all Holocaust themes: Jewish collaboration with the Nazis.

The material discussing Jews cooperating with the Germans to buy either time or favors is ample, and is best consulted in the prodigious scholarship of Holocaust historians.[24] Their investigations explore the work of the *Judenrat,* the Jewish administrative councils that were established to organize and oversee the daily lives of the ghettoized Jewish communities of Europe. The Nazis first appointed and then exploited these groups for their own purposes, although ostensibly they served to make dealing between the two communities less difficult and more efficient. Depending on the city in question or the period of the war, the influence of the *Judenrat* over Jews under its control varied greatly, but the councils were always subservient to the Germans and directly controlled by them. In certain cities, members of the *Judenrat* acted honorably by organizing resistance in numerous, often secret ways while seeming to assist the Nazis. Some were murdered by the Germans for no apparent reason (the irrationality factor again), some chose to take their own lives. In some cities, individual members of the Jewish councils openly collaborated with the Nazis, seeking and obtaining special favors for their families or friends. Members and leaders of the Jewish police forces in the ghettos were gripped by a particularly untenable dilemma from a moral perspective, since they were the most obvious and most capable force for asserting the Germans' will and carrying it out while appearing as the group best able to resist the Nazi mandate.

Playwrights have taken up the sensitive issue of collaboration, creating protagonists whose behavior seems to challenge the possibility of positive images of a kind discussed earlier in plays by Sylvanus, Brady, Wincelberg, or Delbo. They shrink the volitional area of moral action to a space no longer admitting of the "heroic," although most still are reluctant to sacrifice everything to a vision of total foulness. This approach to character and action involves its own kind of risk, and playwrights of these "plays of collaboration" have been accused of betrayal of the victims, nihilism, and even of anti-Semitism. As purveyors of unflattering images of Jews, the authors have usually held to a belief in the ambiguity of moral action that inevitably results in the destruction of all idealized portrayals of character. For theatre audiences, characters who reveal both self-interest *and* moral aspiration create a mixture of dislike and sympathy; in the most extreme cases, where characters have wholly negative personalities, we usually respond with contempt for their actions and rejection of their motives despite a playwright's attempts to have us accept them as also part of the human community.

The character of Mordechai Chaim Rumkowski, protagonist of Harold and Edith Lieberman's *Throne of Straw*,[25] has received much attention for being an apparently negative portrayal of an exceedingly complicated figure. Based on the actual figure of Rumkowski, the head of the Lodz *Judenrat* during the five years that Polish ghetto existed, the central character is a man caught in the trap of collaboration with the enemy, and the playwrights explore the implications of his dilemma. There is evidence that Rumkowski was a ruthless and self-serving tyrant, both petty and cruel, perhaps even mad by the end of his life. But his significance for the Liebermans and for us is that he never loses (in the play, at least) his sense of moral aspiration.

Indisputably, Rumkowski's position was an impossible one. Believing he could make Jewish labor essential to the German war effort, he enthusiastically participated in every plan that would allow the ghetto factories to continue producing, thereby rescuing "his" workers from death. Squeezed between the Nazi chief civilian administrator, Hans Biebow, and the demands of his own suffering people, he experienced a torment in making the required decisions that was surely genuine. In September 1942, he was ordered to arrange the deportation for extermination of the sick, the old, and anyone under the age of ten; this incident provides one of the most terrible moments in the play (act 2, scene 5). His immediate response is to engage the skills he has used more or less successfully in the past with Biebow, the "Jewish" skills of bargaining and negotiating, for which his Nazi boss both appreciates and despises him. But Biebow refuses to change the order (he also has *his* orders, of course), and, in the next scene, one of the two orphan boys is brutally taken away. Thus, in the most graphic way, the question of collaboration with evil is starkly present. Behind it, death lurks everywhere. Eventually, everyone, including Chairman Rumkowski, the Great Collaborator himself, is claimed by it.

To Rumkowski's historical character clings a shameful judgment reserved for those who betray their own people. His character, both historical and theatrical, also exhibits a powerful connection to Jewish folklore and history, and this provides him with an elevated stature not uncommon in traditional tragic characters. In addition, the Liebermans are insistent that Rumkowski's type of personality is a peculiar fixture in European Jewish culture: vain and power-seeking to hide a lack of intellectual confidence, shrewd and opportunistic yet capable of easy charm and great generosity. Nowhere is the archetype more clearly revealed than in the scene with Biebow. First, Rumkowski tries bargaining for a lower deportation age for the children, as Abraham argued with God over the number of righteous to be found in Sodom and Gomorrah, which would enable those cities to be saved. When rebuffed, Rumkowski shows his own deep concern for a positive place in a long, tragic chronicle of Jewish history. "[The children] are my life. And our future. If I do that [agree to the terms of the order], my name would breed maggots. There wouldn't be a single soul who'd say *kaddish* [the prayer for the dead] for me." Later, alone, Rumkowski expresses his feelings directly toward heaven. The stage directions read: "*He looks up, rises and paces back and forth in the following dialog with God. This is not a form of madness—but is part of a long tradition of Jews talking and arguing with Jehovah.*" In addition, Rumkowski's dilemma and his resolution of it are directly related to the teachings of the medieval Jewish philosopher, Maimonides, whose well-known advice on the subject of betrayal and collaboration is quoted in the play and rejected by the Chairman. In these attachments to Jewish history, the Liebermans have created a strong-willed protagonist of a stature and complexity which compares favorably with recognizable tragic protagonists of previous centuries.

Several scenes and two years later, with his power and his will nearly broken, Rumkowski is taunted by Jews he had earlier protected, including his wife, Miriam, and his vicious Chief of Police, Rabinowitz. The small resistance to the final liquidation of the ghetto is neutralized by the Germans with Rumkowski's help (the Liebermans use actual speeches of the Chairman and Biebow at this point in the play), and the final remnant of Lodz's Jewish population is deported for extermination. But the playwrights skillfully direct our attention to the moral implications Rumkowski's dilemma has for the audience concerning the issues of collaboration and complicity. They have dramatized part of the life of a controversial historical figure, and they have continued the controversy in making his actions morally ambiguous and his story theatrically compelling.

The complexity of the human personality, which can draw a person either to goodness or evil in times of extreme stress, is the real subject of this kind of Holocaust drama. Reflecting a tragic conception, the playwrights see their protagonists as gravely flawed, but not without a kind of perverse greatness. In *Throne,* however, they argue not for reclamation of his low reputation, but for an awareness of the confused textures of the human personality, which may issue forth at extreme moments in action that possesses ambiguous dimensions. As a result, they counsel moderation in any posthumous judgment we render. Surrounded by a range of characters who behave either horribly (Gabriel, Rabinowitz) or well (Israel, Miriam), Rumkowski shares with others (Ada, David) a mixture of good and evil that eludes understanding and simple judgment. At the end, the Liebermans force the audience away from an emotional commitment for the suffering victims of the Holocaust through several objectifying (Brechtian) staging devices, but they ungrudgingly accord a measure of respect to a man who, while involved with grievous crimes and responsible for terrible suffering, was always mindful of the moral imperatives of life. Thus, with an astonishing eloquence, he is given time to plead his own tragic case, one not without merit in an ethically shrunken universe.

> First ask yourself where are the other ghettos? Why is it that only mine survives? Because I understood that when the end is good,

everything is good. I won't deny that I had to do terrible things. To give away my poor pigeons. But for every hundred I saved a hundred. I stood as a watchman before the door of death and snatched them from the furnace one by one. *And I am not ashamed.*

(act 2, scene 8)

The life of Jacob Gens, chief of the Vilna Ghetto in Lithuania, was no easier than Rumkowski's in Lodz, but there is some reason to believe that, because of his intelligence and military background, he bore his trial somewhat better, although with no happier result. His career as head of his ghetto was filled with the same moral dilemmas as Rumkowski's, and he too ended up as an ignominious failure. Joshua Sobol's *Ghetto,*[26] like the Liebermans' *Throne,* attempts to tell Gens's story with fairness and sympathy, using similar structural and staging devices. By forcefully dramatizing Gens's career, often using song, dance, extraordinary visual symbolism, and play-within-the-play devices, Sobol is successful in evoking the sense of tragedy often lacking in Holocaust drama.

Ghetto begins in the Tel Aviv apartment of Srulik, a one-armed survivor of the Vilna Ghetto who was the leader of its resident theatre company. Addressing an invisible interviewer, Srulik reflects back on his life, forty years earlier, when his profession allowed him and his troupe certain privileges (including their lives) at the order of Gens. In fact, Gens's attitude toward theatre and all cultural activity in general is both benign and pragmatic: he sees it as a way to raise the morale of the depressed and frightened ghetto inhabitants as well as a way to save more Jews by giving them work. The theatre company actors (and others) assume various additional identities, and they "perform" for the Germans (and, of course, for "us"), thereby lending moments of startling theatricality to a play heavy with ethical speculation.

Gens has two antagonists: Kruk, the ghetto librarian, and Kittel, the corrupt, jazz-loving Nazi, both actual figures in Vilna's history. Although Sobol wants to emphasize the conflict between Gens and Kruk, for theatrical reasons he often returns to Gens *versus* Kittel. There is an additional conflict developed between Kruk and an anti-Semitic German academician, Dr. Paul, who is portrayed by the same actor playing Kittel. But it is Gens who carries the ethical burden of *Ghetto,* and the tragic burden as well.

Sobol's Gens, like the Liebermans' Rumkowski, suffers from the anguish of his impossible position as unquestioned (though not unchallenged) leader of the ghetto. Also like Rumkowski, his life was characterized by the harshness of his authority, the slow compromise of his principles, and the quickness of his wits. Although the moods of despair and hope that seized the ghetto could be frequently reversed by the manipulation of the economic, social, or nutritional conditions he controlled, in truth the political space Gens operated in was exceedingly small. The ghetto he sought to protect through strict adherence to German directives, ameliorated by his own imaginative policies in favor of the young and strong, was doomed by incremental slaughter. In fact, the Vilna Ghetto existed for only a little more than two years (Lodz lasted five), and Gens's death (he was shot by the Gestapo) preceded the ghetto's total liquidation by only a few days. Sobol takes up the ethical issues presented by the act of collaboration and finds in Gens's short, intensely lived career an essentially tragic experience.

Kruk's position in *Ghetto* is that of nay-sayer. He is Gens's mirror image: an idealistic, individualistic, withdrawn intellectual who in the play is frequently accompanied by the sound of a typewriter as he narrates or dictates his diary (actually published in Yiddish in 1961). In their first confrontation, Kruk accuses Gens of trying to appear virtuous when he is really a self-aggrandizing, autocratic traitor. Gens, clearly conscious of his uncertain reputation, responds: "History has yet to judge which of us gave more at this hour of crisis in the history of the Jewish people: you or me!" (act 1, scene 8). Gens's personal sense of his historical place awards him a considerable stature, and, at the same time, lends to his actions a wider, more universal resonance. Later in the play, he is defiant in declaring his objection to Kruk's partiality to satirical-political theatre rather than morale-raising entertainment.

> Not that kind of theater, not the kind that pours salt in our wounds and incites people to rebel. . . . Is this the time for provocation? Theater—by all means. But make people happy. The population here needs to be calm, disciplined, industrious. . . . Objectively speaking, you are traitors! . . . If there's anyone with a genuine national sentiment in this ghetto, it's me! If there's a real Jewish patriot and nationalist here, it's me!
>
> (act 3, scene 1)

Of course, there is a self-serving point to Gens's anger, too: a more passive population will reduce the threat to his authority.

Still, Sobol retains for Gens a large measure of sympathy while Gens struggles with his antagonists to justify his eminently worthwhile goal: to keep alive as many Jews as possible until the certain defeat of the Germans. His actions, sentencing some Jews to death while bargaining to keep others alive, are simultaneously laudable and contemptible. His drunken concluding speech (Gens's actual words) in act 2, where he "*seems to be responding to the voice of Kruk,*" is shattering in its logic, terrifying in its eloquence.

> Many of you consider me a traitor and many of you are wondering what I'm still doing here, among innocent and immaculate souls like yourselves. . . . I, Gens, give orders to blow up hideaways that you prepared, and I, Gens, try to figure out ways of protecting Jews from death. I do the reckoning of Jewish blood, not of Jewish dignity. If the Germans ask me for one thousand Jews, I give them what they want because if we don't do it ourselves, the Germans will come and take the people by force. And then they wouldn't take one thousand, but thousands. Thousands. You with your sanctimonious morality. You don't deign to touch the filth. And if you do survive, you'll be able to say: we came out of it with a clear conscience, while I, Jacob Gens, if I have the good fortune of getting out of this alive, I'll be covered in slime, my hands will be dripping with blood. Nevertheless, I'd be prepared to stand trial, to submit to Jewish justice. I would get up and say: whatever I did was meant to save as many Jews as I could, to lead them to freedom. In order for some of them to be spared I had no choice but to lead others to their death with my very own hands. And in order to spare some Jews their clear conscience I had no choice but to plunge into the filth, leaving my own conscience behind.[27]
>
> (act 2, scene 4)

Gens is surrounded by people who span the full range of the Jewish response to oppression. Dessler and Mushkat (Jewish police), Weiskopf (Jewish profiteer), and several Jewish gangster-murderers represent the negative extreme; Hayya (an actress and singer) and Srulik (ventriloquist and puppeteer), the positive. Gens is defined by the moral position he takes between them, and thus he is often a picture of melancholy confusion (as Kittel notes) whose torment is genuine and whose dilemma is insoluble. Only when *Ghetto* takes up the more philosophical, subsidiary theme of the nature of the Jewish soul does its theatrical power diminish somewhat. (Sobol deals with that theme more forcefully in his companion play written around the same time, *Soul of a Jew.*) Nonetheless, for its audacious theatricality and scenic effects (the dominant visual image is a ten-foot-high pile of clothing at stage center representing Jewish occupations, Jewish enslavement,

Jewish accommodation, and Jewish destruction), for its provocative
intellectual debate of crucial moral issues, and especially for its grip-
ping image of an aspiring, guilty, doomed protagonist, Ghetto makes a
significant claim to finding true tragedy in the Holocaust experience.

IV

What then can be said of the tragic "response" of audiences in the
presence of these plays? There are many paradoxes associated with
tragedy in the theatre, not the least of which is our attraction to seeing
other people suffer in the expectation that some profit (catharsis? insight?) will be derived. Receiving and assimilating the knowledge of six
million dead depends on the ability of the playwright to portray
historical reality and at the same time to force from us a deep emotional
response that touches upon our own sense of survival. In modern
times, romantic postures and optimistic creeds have been inferior to
portrayals of terrible dilemmas and ambiguous truths in human history
and behavior. Nonetheless, despite the irreparable, catastrophic result
of the Holocaust, despair is rarely total, in part because some did survive the genocidal frenzy, and in part because these playwrights cannot
accept unmitigated negation. (An exception may be several of the
contemporary German playwrights I discuss in chapter 5.)

When the traditional tragic protagonists concluded their painful
careers, they were touched by discovery; through them audiences received an illumination that diminished (slightly? temporarily?) the
dark components (ignorance? evil?) of human existence. Writers of
tragedy have always had to calibrate this balance of gain amid loss with
extreme care. Making audiences accept themselves, if only for the span
of a theatrical performance, as the living legacy of the Holocaust
presents enormous challenges for the playwright who must cope with
the contraction in the freedom to maneuver demanded by history. But
the mysteries at the heart of human existence that tragedy has always
tried to convey have never disappeared, and neither has the attempt to
write tragedy in the theatre. Lawrence Langer, writing about how, in
images of the concentration camps, "affirmation includes negation,"[28]
was inevitably writing about the opposite condition: these plays call
out for us to realize that negation also includes affirmation.

Three

The (Tragi)Comic Vision

So the theatre has the task of expressing, symbolizing, and
representing how, in the face of or the threat of extinction, one
imagines human continuity.

—Robert J. Lifton
"Art and the Imagery of Extinction"

Oᴜʀ instinctual feeling that comedy and the Holocaust are incompatible is appropriate but mistaken in light of the theatrical evidence at
hand. Although it would be difficult to find a Holocaust play that
could be called a comedy, it is easy to find plays on the Holocaust
theme that use comic strategies to make their points, one of which
surely is to help show the terror of the Holocaust. This kind of Holocaust drama may involve comic characters, structures, or viewpoints
that, in the context of history, provoke startling and controversial responses; a review of comic theory and of some of these plays shows
why.

It is by now commonplace to analyze comic form in terms of its
tragic opposite, and critics frequently compare the two to better understand each of them. Most modern critics agree, however, that comedy
can only appear *after* tragedy has been in evidence so as to present an
alternative to the tragic vision or to comment upon it. "Comedy seems
not only to follow tragedy," writes Walter Kerr, "but to derive from
it,"[1] by which he means that our dominant vision of life is serious, but
that comedy is a "drag or reminder" that other perspectives on life are
possible because the tragic perspective is, by itself, incomplete. This
relationship of comedy as a dependent aspect of tragedy and often a

commentator on it, is relevant to one way in which comedy is used in Holocaust drama.

Subscribing to even this contingent relationship requires a decision that not all playwrights can make: to see the Holocaust as tragic in the first place, providing material for tragic plays. I have noted elsewhere that many dramatists and critics *reject* tragedy as an artistic option because they cannot extract from the historical evidence any *meaning* that would allow the Holocaust experience to be transcended. From the murder of six million Jews *no* positive message can be discerned, they say, and to imply that one is possible is to impose a romantic and sentimental (and morally offensive) vision of an unredeemed and unredeemable event. To them, the Holocaust is the incontrovertible validation of our unheroic age, impossible to be enriched or ennobled, merely to be recorded with a maximum of respect for the victims and a minimum of authorial interference. Of course these writers, and others as well, reject a comic perspective on the Holocaust, too.

However the Holocaust may exist in the minds of playwrights, it nevertheless exists in history as an irreparable, ineffaceable event. For playwrights who do engage the Holocaust experience, the pressure of history enforces an essential seriousness on the circumstances to be explained and the situations to be retold. All playwrights (and audiences) would agree that the most objectionable approach to the Holocaust in both a moral as well as aesthetic sense is the frivolous one, i.e., of viewing the events unseriously and of treating the victims disrespectfully. There is, however, no sure agreement as to what constitutes a frivolous treatment, and there is much disagreement among critics and audiences concerning plays whose incorporation of comic elements seems to show this attitude, whether or not the playwright intended to. The great absurdist playwright, Eugene Ionesco, about whom more will be said, may have summed up (and avoided) the issue best in his implied request for a less formal approach to drama: "It all comes to the same thing anyway; comic and tragic are merely two aspects of the same situation, and I have reached the stage when I find it hard to distinguish one from the other."[2]

Robert Corrigan has written about how "comedy is negative in its definition," i.e., operable only after tragedy defines the standards that comedy seeks to oppose. He has also spoken of how, in comedy, "death is never taken seriously or even considered as a serious threat."[3] For obvious reasons, this viewpoint is impossible to sustain completely in dramas of the Holocaust, where death is everywhere and unavoidable. Thus, the appearance of comedy in Holocaust drama is often intrusive and reflexive, calling attention to itself by admitting the futility of its own function, which is, as Susanne Langer has noted, the assertion of life's vital continuity, "organic unity, growth and self-preservation,"[4] with some chance for success. "The action of comedy moves toward a deliverance,"[5] writes Northrop Frye, but *we know before the curtain rises* that, in most cases, deliverance was absent during the Holocaust. In this kind of Holocaust drama, then, comedy is vested in selected individual characters whose very presence complements and deepens the essential seriousness of the plays. No matter how terrible life is, these characters are always "good for a laugh."

The theatre of the Holocaust, however, does not always deal with the victims of the Holocaust, or at least its dead ones, and often they become the focus of a second kind of comic Holocaust drama. In choosing *not* to focus on those who were murdered, playwrights make an artistic decision that enables them to engage a more formal comic option in the theatre, and to define a situation influenced by, but not subsumed into, a picture of unrelieved grimness. Just as some writers search in Holocaust history for tragic materials and concentrate on the "heroic" examples of human behavior in inhumane times, other writers defy the terminal pressure of history by considering the survivors of the Holocaust. In doing so, they do not ignore the terrible result of Hitler's genocidal "final solution," but they divert our attention from it by asking us to attend to the experience of those who lived through the terror. Here again, we note comedy's contingent status since, even in dealing with survivors, death must be acknowledged before it is transcended. Nevertheless, these plays are emptied of the comic emotion of joy (in Eric Bentley's formulation) and despite deliverance, a mournful quality often remains. (Even here, we must pause and reassess the evidence of survival in Holocaust history, if only to remember that four of the greatest Holocaust writers—Borowski, Celan, Amery, and, most recently, Primo Levi—like countless other survivors of the concentration camps, committed suicide many years after their "liberation.")

A strategy of dealing with survivors in Holocaust drama permits the creation of a world of romance (as Frye explains it), where a new world is established, although it rests on the ashes of the old; it is a conscience-stricken kind of comedy that "has taken note," in Bentley's phrase, one that "takes place on the other side of despair."[6] Admittedly, this kind of comedy is based on a perception of aesthetic form that is comic in the sense that life is seen to go on despite obstacles to its continuance. For at the heart of traditional comic form there is an affirmation of life, along with the understanding that future obstacles to survival will be overcome. Comedy in these dramas is found in the playwright's vision.

There is a third way in which comedy appears in Holocaust drama, not as an intrusion on tragedy or as an image of continuance, but as a fully expressed antithesis to the seriousness of the Holocaust. Here, playwrights advance a comic vision *in spite of the tragedy,* defying its purity and its dominance. This kind of comedy challenges tragedy, not in its catastrophic nature but in the overall seriousness of its action and spirit. These plays turn comedy against itself, often in the style of parody, insisting on an equality with the tragic viewpoint and rejecting subordinate status. Their objective is to shock audiences from complacency and somber respectfulness. Ostensibly, these plays even go so far as to mock the Holocaust experience and make grotesque fun of the victims' suffering. Their impact derives from a combination of revulsion and outrageousness that frequently conceals an underlying ethical passion. The modern expression of this form of comedy is often noted in the theatre of the absurd, where serious issues are treated comically in order to repel audiences, so that the subsequent impact is that much greater. A shamelessness and aggression in these playwrights' work contradicts our theatrical expectations. Their plays seem to exploit the Holocaust experience by taking advantage of the audience's emotional preference for optimism, rationality, and self-satisfaction. The master of absurdist technique, Ionesco, is quoted in Martin Esslin's book *The Theatre of the Absurd* as having said: ". . . the comic alone is capable of giving us the strength to bear the tragedy of existence. The true nature of things, truth itself, can be revealed to us only by fantasy, which is more realistic than all the realisms."[7]

As noted above, the comic vision allows for a recognition of terrible historical facts, but, in this third way of introducing comedy into the Holocaust story, what is sought is neither a "deepening" of the seriousness through contrast with "lighter" moments or "funny" characters, nor a hopeful vision of future possibility, however tentatively advanced, but rather an explosive confrontation of comic and tragic forms as a way to energize our depressed responses. In exploiting our tendency toward seriousness and respect for the Holocaust and its victims, this approach arouses audiences in ways that more traditional comic devices or perspectives cannot. It is a method that most playwrights of the Holocaust shun. These plays take the greatest chances by their provocative use of dramatic form and are the most difficult to perform and to accept. But when they succeed, their effect is powerfully felt because of their reliance on a clash, rather than a harmony, of the tragic and comic.

In the broadest sense, what is under discussion here is the *mixture* of comedy and tragedy that has evolved over the course of this century, a way of writing for the theatre that David Hirst calls our "dominant dramatic form," tragicomedy.[8] Because of enormous changes in our self-image and self-understanding (the result of the twentieth-century developments in psychology, sociology, theology, and politics), we have come to accept as generally plausible and accurate a vision of the human condition that is best conveyed through an impure dramatic form. Eric Bentley distinguishes two basic kinds of tragicomedies and comments on their historical appearance: "The comedy with a tragic sequel—or tragedy with a comic substructure—probably could not have come into its own until the rise of Naturalism with its insistence that happy endings do not occur in real life."[9] And although the mixture of forms can be identified in plays prior to the late nineteenth century (Hirst locates its origins in the sixteenth century, Kerr finds it in Sophoclean Greece), certainly the shocks and stresses of the twentieth century, in their cumulative and comprehensive impact, permanently altered the way in which we look at ourselves in our theatre.[10]

On the one hand, the Holocaust, in the sheer magnitude of its destruction and the incomprehensibility of its motive, can be credited with administering the ultimate blow to humane and meaningful images of human society. On the other, the Holocaust may have forced our bruised and grudging imaginations to seek artistic images that can validate, though certainly not guarantee, survival. "The fuel of hope is innocence," Paul Fussell has written in *The Great War and Modern Memory,* but for some the Holocaust has consumed all hope by destroying innocent possibility. For them, plays that hold out *any* hope are irresponsible as well as deceptive, and provoke responses that cheat the victims of their dignity and separate despair from its truth.[11] Yet, as the detained LeDuc admits in Arthur Miller's Holocaust play *Incident at Vichy:* "It's just that you keep finding these little shreds of hope, and it's difficult. . . ." One artistic answer to this aesthetic and ethical dilemma may be found in the tragicomic form, not in the sense that it reconciles these opposites but that it exemplifies the closeness of their essential natures. In Bentley's words (and not without a final demur), tragicomedy "is a challenge to despair [that] has addressed itself to the peculiarly harrowing, withering despairs of our epoch. Whatever one may say of it, one cannot say it does not get down to the bedrock. Real

hope can be found only through real despair—short of the latter's being
so 'real,' so utter, that it swallows us up."[12]

I

One of the traditional functions of comedy, certainly of Jewish
comedy, is to alleviate the pain of existence by finding laughter in the
most hurtful situations. Making us laugh at our troubles has been the
honorable work of the comedian now and throughout theatre history.
At the same time, the comic figure serves to decrease the sense of
threat, often by offering himself up for abuse or ridicule, or, alter-
nately, by directing laughter at others deserving of scorn for their
pretension or folly. Frequently comic characters cling to an outlook on
life that refutes dour reality with a contagious energy and a circumspect
stance. Yet, the comic posture, however adversarial, is essentially con-
servative, drawing wayward energies back into the mainstream of behavior, where continuance and compromise become possible. Because
both are hardly possible in the context of the Holocaust, the comic
character carries, along with his resistance to authority, a burden of
futility that is impossible to put down. In the comic characters of Holocaust drama we encounter a mechanism for the temporary diversion
from harm in a representative figure whose indomitability is only
slightly smaller than his desperation and his foreclosed future.

Although they differ in many respects, Millard Lampell's dramatization of John Hersey's novel *The Wall* (1960)[13] and Harold and
Edith Lieberman's *Throne of Straw* (1978)[14] share an identical story
(the destruction of a ghetto) and a similar comic strategy. The worlds
of the two plays are entirely Jewish, and both describe the physical and
spiritual degradation of the once extensive and vibrant Jewish culture
of Poland. Each play contains a major comic character who serves to
deepen the sadness and anger that dominate the emotional response of
the audience. Additionally, through the behavior and perspective of
the comic character, the plays are able to augment the audience's feelings with an additional, if not alternate, response: pride (*The Wall*)
and thoughtfulness (*Throne of Straw*).

In *The Wall*, the comic mantle is worn mostly by the peddler Fishel
Shpunt. Act 1, in fact, begins with a wholly comic bit of business, as
Shpunt, with great difficulty, carries an oversized chair from the apartment house to the ghetto street and eventually to his cart. The stage
direction describes this action in terms that disguise the seriousness of
his work: the need people have to sell their furniture in order to secure

money for food. The comic opening also conceals the seriousness of the play as a whole, which is a dramatic retelling of the destruction of the Warsaw Ghetto.

An ornate chair emerges from the house. A pair of staggering human legs leads to the suspicion that buried somewhere beneath it is a man.

The chair is jostled and the hidden "man" protests, after which

*The chair teeters and falls with a crash, revealing a scowling gnome—*FISHEL SHPUNT. SHPUNT'S *face has a magnificent ugliness. It is more than a face—it is a mask of tragedy, giving a certain grandeur to this little man in his battered coat.* SHPUNT *regards life with habitual suspicion and fury, as though it were an old enemy forever trying to swindle him.*

The dialogue that follows this description underscores Shpunt's function in the play: to provide a kind of comical wisdom, won by adversity in life, that serves as counterpoint to the more serious action to come. In fact, the whole first scene is weighted toward the comic, a mood abetted by the music of a distant carousel, which, as with Shpunt himself, gradually comes to take a more grim place in the play's opening act. In scene 3, Shpunt is selected by a German sergeant and ordered to dance in the street in front of a group of mourners. He gives a performance grotesque in the extreme, at once comic and humiliating, concluding with Shpunt looking "like a wounded bird." Later, Shpunt will repeat the "*hopping jig, a weird, froglike gavotte,*" as a kind of trademark, proof, as another character says, that "since the day they broke up the prayer meeting, he isn't right in the head." In his "unbalanced" condition, Shpunt fills his place in the play as a wise fool, altering the tone of the scenes he appears in with witty song as well as clumsy dance. He exits the first scene in act 2, "crooning" a lullaby and wearing a bizarre wig, comically underscoring the desperate situation of the Jews behind the ghetto wall.

As the play advances, Shpunt's character continues to undergo a transformation toward the more serious. As his true madness increases, his comic function becomes less of a dramaturgical option, and his appearances are less frequent as the play's action (preparing and executing the Warsaw uprising) takes precedence over its atmosphere. Later, comic counterpoint is provided by Berson, the eventual "hero" of *The Wall,* who greatly differs from Shpunt because he does not take the ghetto communal situation seriously, preferring the attitude of

selfish indifference to his fellow Jews' predicament, an attitude occasionally expressed through the music of his cheery concertina. Until the
final scene, when Berson is converted by love and anger to aggressive
resistance, his attitude is one of distant mockery, for which he is
strongly rebuked by Rachel Apt, one of the ghetto fighters.

> BERSON: . . . What an amazing thing man is. He can bear the
> unbearable. (RACHEL rises.) Rachel . . . (RACHEL whirls and slaps
> his face.) What's that for?
> RACHEL: For being a liar! For that lying smile. Because you
> know . . . trying to warn them wasn't ridiculous. Didn't you?
> BERSON: Yes.
> RACHEL: But you wouldn't say it. You had to pretend, stand
> there grinning, turn it into a farce. Why couldn't you say it?
> BERSON: Because it's impossible to convince warm healthy
> human beings that they're going to die. Even if I'd agreed with
> you, it wouldn't have made any difference.
> RACHEL: It would have made a difference to me.
>
> (act 2, scene 5)

In the last act of The Wall, Shpunt's character also changes again,
assuming several functions that are not entirely consistent with each
other. He continues to serve as a kind of street comedian, performing
demented parodies of the Nazis and exercising, when possible, his
mordant wit. After he is taken away for deportation by the Germans,
we expect he will disappear from the play. But he reappears in the final
scene in the besieged bunker, all the more miraculously because the
"battered gnome" has been transformed into a fighting partisan, clear-
headed and disciplined, who leads the few surviving fighters of the
revolt out of their hideout in search of freedom on the other side of the
ghetto wall. For unspecified reasons, he no longer appears crazy, and,
we note, he is no longer comic, either; his kind of comedy now has no
place in The Wall. For much of the play he has asserted the humor of
the outsider, varying the tone of the drama and complementing its
darkness. But in the final scene we see death defied with serious, not
comic, action: the last Yiddish song makes this clear (as does the last
stage direction). In the character of Shpunt we recognize most clearly
the comic method whereby the production can be both lightened and
deepened, and can provide to audiences (according to the playwright) a
fuller picture of the ghetto's inhabitants, who possess "a tenement ex-
uberance . . . mirrored in their humor—their sardonic, bold, bitter-
sweet mockery of themselves."[15]

The character of Yankele in *Throne of Straw* closely resembles Shpunt, but the Liebermans have created him with an additional theatrical dimension that makes him markedly different in dramatic function. Yankele carries a dual responsibility in the play, serving as both character and narrator. In other words, he fulfills a Brechtian function, stepping in and out of the action, guiding our attention to moral questions while maintaining a stance of *double* outsider, i.e., someone who confronts the community in the play *and* the audience watching the play. His costume and behavior differentiate him from the other characters: he is a Hasid (an orthodox Jew), spiritual and obsessed, rather than pragmatic and occasionally observant like his coreligionists. In addition, he is intended to represent a purer version of central Europe's Jewish-Yiddish culture, the simpler, old-world lifestyle that was destroyed by the Nazis.

Yankele, as the playwrights note, is both a witness and a storyteller. His observations during the course of the play reflect his "Yiddish world view," which Mark Shechner describes as "to domesticate the exalted and cut the marvelous and the awesome down to human scale."[16] This description is apt for Yankele's brand of comedy in *Throne of Straw*, which is motivated by the just revenge of the weak on the powerful. When combined with his tendency to madness (which supplies further motivation), Yankele is able to present an emotional alternative to the play's grim action, an alternative that breaks the audience's involvement through laughter. Early in the play, Yankele meets Mordechai Rumkowski in the street and, in the presence of others, gleefully mocks the pretentions and authority of the Chairman of the Lodz *Judenrat*.

> ADA *(boldly)*: Mr. Chairman, to put it plainly, my family could use some help.
> RUMKOWSKI: That's just what I'm in a position to do.
> YANKELE: Yes. We've seen the position. (*Laughs.* RABINOWITZ *starts for him.*)
> RUMKOWSKI: Rabinowitz, let me handle this.
> YANKELE: Please let him, for he can handle anything. (*Dances around* RUMKOWSKI.) Court Jew, Council Jew. Do you think you can pull us through this time? Oh yes, Commandant Biebow. I can do this. I can do that. I can do everything. And Rabinowitz will oblige.
> RUMKOWSKI: Must you make a fool of yourself in public?
> YANKELE: So you don't fool the public and yourself? You know,

I wanted to be Chairman myself, but I didn't know what to
promise.

(act 1, scene 2)

Yankele's temper is, in Shechner's phrase, "humor as the Jews have
long known it, an attitude that lies perilously close to desperation as
laughter for them is always close to tears."[17]

With Chairman Rumkowski as his antagonist, Yankele has a splendid target for his caustic observations. (In fact, many characters in
Throne have occasional opportunity to employ the same kind of defla-
tionary self-mockery, which adds linguistic texture to the Liebermans'
Jewish environment.) Yankele's comic contribution to the play is further expressed by his presentational function outside the story. His
three grimly comic songs, "Courting the Jews," "A Homage to Rumkowski," and "The Riddle Song," which all deal with the increasingly
desperate situation in the ghetto, are all directed to the audience, forcing viewers to adjust their emotional response and, at the same time, to
recognize the double way in which comedy operates in *Throne*: as a
distraction in the play from the terror of the ghetto situation and as a
mechanism to insure an objective perspective on the moral implications
of the Holocaust experience. Yankele, and other characters like him in
Holocaust drama, is one of Susanne Langer's "important comic per-
sonage[s] . . . tumbling and stumbling from one situation to another,
getting into scrape after scrape. . . ."[18] but with this difference: Yankele
exists to tell us that most of the people like himself didn't survive the
final scrape of the "final solution." Yankele survives the destruction of
the ghetto but (as he says) only in order to carry a tragicomic legacy: to
make us feel, through bitter laughter, the irreparability of the human
loss of the Holocaust and the impossibility of making easy judgments
about it.

C. P. Taylor's *Good* (1981) and Theodore Herstand's *The Emigration of Adam Kurtzik* (1986) reveal tragicomic strategies similar to
those of *The Wall* and *Throne of Straw*, but they extend the "Jew as
Outsider" image by placing the Jewish characters in non-Jewish en-
vironments where they are despised and abused. In Taylor's play, the
object of our interest is Maurice, the only Jew in the play and,
significantly, the best friend of the Nazi protagonist, Halder. In Herstand's play, the protagonist, Kurtzik, does interact with other Jews,
but the dominant action of the play lies in his relationship to his Nazi
persecutors. Both characters, initially presented comically, eventually
meet their inevitable, terrible destiny.

In his brief author's note, Taylor elucidates his concern with questions of theatrical genre: "What the tragedy which I have written as a comedy, or *musical comedy* is about, will hopefully emerge in the performance. If it proves the good play we hope it is, like all good plays, it will have special meaning, or shade of meaning, for each person who experiences it."[19] Nonetheless, Taylor knows the meaning the Holocaust has for him: it stands as the most powerful historical proof of the murderous result of human indifference, which all of us, in some way, possess. According to Taylor, it is indifference that is responsible for atrocities past and present, and that will be the cause of the "final solution to end all final solutions . . . nuclear holocaust." Himself of Jewish descent, Taylor sees in the story of Holocaust Jewry the best case-study of the world's previous ethical failures; in observing the way Jews were treated by the Nazis and the way others remained largely indifferent, he finds a standard of measure for evil in the modern world.

Good alerts us to the need for ethical vigilance and rededication. The play is a denunciation of people who drift without moral standards, who believe that actions have no lasting repercussions and that active opposition to evil is unnecessary. It is Taylor's special achievement to have fashioned a play in which comedy (or musical comedy) reveals so much of the tragedy of history. (The play takes place between 1933 and 1942.) In *Good,* the main comic character is (in Taylor's terms) the truly tragic one: the Jew whose presence is both a reminder of and an irritant to Professor Halder's amoral self.

Maurice, a psychiatrist, is the play's consummate outsider: a Jew who dislikes most other Jews. He is comic in his traditional attempt to adapt to his increasingly desperate situation. His intelligence continually refutes his optimism that the persecution of Jews will stop, and, caught between what he knows and what he wants to believe, he is a bundle of nervous contradictions, never more so than in his use of vulgar language for expressing two common components of Jewish humor: anxiety and skepticism.[20]

> It's a basic biological drive, you see, Johnnie . . . When people come after you with fucking machine guns, you start running . . . Look at me . . . I'm calm. I'm looking at this cold and rationally . . . Yes . . . It's a temporary aberration . . . The trouble is, with all the machine guns in this fucking country, it's not going to take all that long a temporary aberration to finish off the whole Jewish population . . .
>
> (act 2, ellipses in text)

He pleads for help from his friend Halder but is abandoned to a certain death as Halder (and others) take up the theme of "blaming the victim" for their troubles. "What's he saying?" asks Maurice. "What's this shithead talking about? It's my fault his fucking machine guns mowed me down?" Gradually, Maurice comes to recognize that he too has compromised and adapted for too long, finally jeopardizing his very life. Filled with his own insecurities and prejudices, he is a psychiatric figure of fun, although still an innocent victim and, so far as the crimes of the Third Reich are concerned, wholly blameless. Midway through the play, when Halder has one of his last pangs of conscience, Maurice persists in expressing the terror of his situation comically; the scene takes place in a public park in the middle of winter, where Halder and Maurice hold clandestine meetings.

> MAURICE *(handing him a parcel)*: I brought you some cheesecake . . . Where will you get Jewish cheesecake, when you've locked up all the Jews?
> HALDER *(alarmed)*: Is that somebody coming? Somebody's coming. Feed the pigeons, Maurice.
> MAURICE: Nobody's coming . . .
> HALDER: Feed the pigeons, Maurice . . .
> MAURICE: I've nothing to feed the fucking pigeons with!
> HALDER: *(offering the cheesecake)*: Here. Give them some cheesecake.
> MAURICE: I'm not feeding good, Jewish cheesecake to fucking *pigeons!*
> HALDER: There is somebody coming.
> MAURICE: They've come to listen to your band. It's an unusual attraction for the park in winter. [. . .] That cheesecake. I bought it at Epstein's. I can't *stand* them. I can't stand *Jews*. I spent thirty-five Marks in there at one go, and they couldn't even give me a "good afternoon" . . . You're right. There's something seriously wrong with Jews. I can see Hitler's point.
>
> (act 2)

Taylor's moral concerns are strongly tied to the form of his play, which, he specifies in his subtitle, *is* a tragedy. In *Good,* adaptive comic behavior is a useless tactic insofar as Maurice uses it to soften the reality of the evil that surrounds him. As the play advances chronologically, the laughter he evokes in the play gets more desperate and the tragic inevitability becomes much more apparent to the audience. Thus, musical comedy form impinges directly on the somber theme of *Good,* and Maurice's attempt at compromise and evasion, which in a less threatening situation would be comic behavior, in the Holocaust context produces a dangerous, tragicomic response. Thematically speaking, failure to take a stand, refusing to resist the presence of evil *is* the tragedy of our modern age, according to Taylor. In other words, accommodating to and accepting new definitions of "good" is both a ludicrous and risky exercise of moral relativism.

Taylor's comic approach to his serious theme incorporates music for its effects, as he indicates in his author's note. The dance band and vocalists on stage throughout *Good* play and sing mostly cheerful romantic songs, and, like Maurice, serve to counterpoint the action tonally. The music serves several functions: to provide entertainment for the audience, to comment ironically on the action, to increase the suspense of the play by retarding the chronological progress of the story, to provide motivation and distraction for Halder (the band Maurice refers to in his conversation in the park is the "imaginary" music that caused Halder to seek Maurice's professional advice), and to supply a brilliant *coup de théâtre* as the band members turn into the ragged concentration camp orchestra discordantly playing a Schubert march to welcome Halder to his new job as camp commandant. "The band was *real,*" are Halder's last words, an acknowledgment that there is a certain point beyond which we can no longer delude ourselves that we are not responsible for monstrous evil.

Several of these musical functions appear at a point early in *Good* when Halder and his unstable, guilt-ridden wife sing in recitative to each other, accompanied by a café trio. The entertainment value of the scene conflicts with the occasionally serious message in the lyrics, producing an extraordinary tension that is the distinguishing feature of Taylor's dramaturgy in this play. When the music is upbeat, sentimental, and romantic, it serves as a distraction for Halder from his moral decline; for the audience it serves as a distraction from the seriousness of Taylor's story about moral decline, until finally "distraction" becomes the theme itself.

When Hitler appears to Halder as a street musician playing a Yiddish folksong, we can laugh at the grotesque nature and sound of the event. But Taylor's point is that we delude ourselves to the real nature of the world's evil and that, unlike Halder, we must learn to discriminate sooner between the serious Führer and the comic Charlie Chaplin with whom Halder confuses him—and then we must act on that knowledge. Until we discern what is truly evil, our terror of annihilation can be escaped only if we become complicitous in the killing of others. Taylor's musical comedy is of the most serious sort, a frightening tragicomic portrayal of two human beings, one unwise to be comic and the other unable to be serious.

The Emigration of Adam Kurtzik[21] begins as a satirical comedy that, in its second half, moves deliberately closer to a tragic vision. Theodore Herstand's play provides a tragicomic portrait of the Holocaust experience from the perspective of a "little man" (kurz is German for "brief" or "short"), an Everyman (Adam) who is caught up in terrible circumstances he cannot understand or control. The Emigration is, in part, a refutation of the Holocaust seen as tragedy, or at least heroically. The play's protagonist is clearly an antihero, and the action of the play is, for much of its length, comic in tone and conception. Nonetheless, the seriousness of Kurtzik's situation is never far from the audience's understanding, even in the play's comic scenes. Thus, in the first scene, Kurtzik is summoned to the office of one of the Nazi officers who has jurisdiction over his town, whereupon he naturally sits on a chair to wait for his appointment to begin. Immediately, Kurtzik receives a "hard, stinging" slap across the face from the German clerk. The violent gesture is one from which neither Kurtzik nor the audience ever fully recovers; its effect is to put us emotionally off balance.

Unlike the Liebermans' Rumkowski or Sobol's Jacob Gens, who are figures of stature and some limited influence, Kurtzik, head of the Jewish Council in his small Polish town, remains the picture of confusion and ineffectuality. He is, in essence, the Elder as Shlemiehl.[22] In creating this kind of tragicomic image, Herstand is both courageous and unusual. The play's initial premise contradicts our usual expectations of Holocaust characterization. Act 1 is composed of a series of encounters between Kurtzik and three different pairs of Nazi functionaries. They are all played by the same two actors, who change only a hat or coat to alter their identities; they all inhabit the same "interchangeable" office space (which, in fact, serves as Kurtzik's office too). Kurtzik's bafflement at their identical appearance and contradictory orders, and his attempt to reconcile their conflicting demands, provide a comic, episodic structure for the first half of the play. The comedy is greatly enhanced (and our expectations further disturbed) because Kurtzik's personality makes him totally unfit for the serious role thrust on him. He confronts the Nazis' interchangeable malevolence with a bedraggled, dogged equanimity. He lacks even a self-deprecating wit to enhance his character. Much is made of Kurtzik's fastidiousness and denial of his Jewishness, and little is provided him in the way of charm, let alone courage. As Bentley reminds us, the comic virtue is "tenacity, by which men survive,"[23] except that Poland's Kurtziks, as Holocaust drama recognizes, rarely did.

Kurtzik's character does undergo a transformation as the action of the play shifts from the relative safety of 1939 to the disastrous 1942. Act 2 begins surprisingly with a grotesque two-man vaudeville sketch satirizing Hitler and Kurtzik himself in his position as council chairman, performed by two distinguished actors from the ghetto in heavy Yiddish accents.[24] Kurtzik arrives and orders the cabaret canceled, although with sadness and apologies. (The audience is the sketch's "audience.") After the skit ends, Kurtzik is viciously beaten by two Nazi soldiers, an event that marks a turning point in Kurtzik's character. He begins to receive considerable sympathy from the audience, the result of his pain's seeming *real* and thus no longer comic. He is lifted to his feet and slowly exits with the funny remark: "You wouldn't believe the headache I have." The next scene is mostly a long and overly dramatic monolog from Kurtzik's complaining wife, Felicia, and contains two surprises: first, the discovery that the body in their bed to whom she speaks is not Adam but Schwartz (they alternate sleeping in the one bed in their apartment), and second, that Schwartz, the object of her verbal abuse, is dead.

As the threat of deportation and death grows, Kurtzik's character changes and deepens. Mercilessly preyed upon, he finally seems to have accumulated enough wisdom through suffering and left behind much of his foolishness and gullibility. Three years of ghetto existence have at last incited him to plan two acts that could almost be called courageous: warning the Jewish community of the Nazis' plans for its destruction, and committing suicide. But, as befits a shlemiehl, his plans go awry: first, the Germans act too quickly for the community to be warned, and second, the pill that Uncle Kaplan has promised would cause instant death is bogus. He takes the drug, puts his head on the desk, and waits for the end.

> KAPLAN: Kurtzik! I can't get to the printers! And to see Felicia, impossible! The streets are full of soldiers! (KAPLAN *stops, dead in his tracks.*) Kurtzik! Oh, my God! The pills! (KURTZIK *slowly lifts his head. He gazes forward.*) Oy! For a minute, I thought . . . Such a scare you gave me!

KURTZIK (*Simply as he holds the small bottle and looks at it.*):
They didn't work.
KAPLAN: You took one?
KURTZIK: I took two.
KAPLAN: They didn't do anything?
KURTZIK: Nothing.
KAPLAN: Katz [the seller of the pills], when I see him, I'll kill
him.

(act 2, scene 8)

Finally, Kurtzik is marched off, a comic figure caught in a tragic
fate, a tragicomic image of the Holocaust experience. Herstand takes
up the story of the destruction of the ordinary Jews of Europe and
purges it of heroism. The satirical thrust of the first act distracts us
from the overall seriousness of the situation, and the play seems suspended until intermission, not yet ready to declare itself or its intentions. At the play's conclusion, Herstand's attitude toward the ethical
issues is entirely certain, full of sadness and anger, and leaving us with
an image of cold brutality, which is all the more forbidding without the
warmth of his unfortunate comic protagonist. By the end of the second
act, *The Emigration of Adam Kurtzik* has explored a full range of emo-
tions, tragicomically, with great theatrical skill.

II

Two plays that stress the idea of continuity by their concern with
characters who inherit the memory of a destroyed world and a vision of
a newly created one are Lea Goldberg's *Lady of the Castle* (1956)[25] and
Jean-Claude Grumberg's *The Workroom* (1979).[26] Goldberg's play
takes place in 1947 and deals with a young Jewish woman who has
been hidden from the Nazis during the war by the caretaker of a castle
located somewhere in central Europe. The play describes the way both
must confront the need to start a new life, which, in the woman's case,
involves her being convinced to emigrate to Palestine. (Goldberg, a
noted Israeli poet, emigrated from Europe to Palestine in 1935 and
died in 1970.) The play combines a Chekhovian theme (the ambivalence and confusion that accompany the replacement of an old
order with a new, brash one) with an Ibsenesque melodramatic structure.[27] At the play's conclusion, the woman, guided by the advice of the
two emissaries from Palestine ("We only care about one thing: that this
girl should begin living again the normal life of girls her age . . . she's

got to decide whether she'll choose a free, decent life, without fear and deceit . . .") chooses life in the Middle East, although at the price of her fantastic imagination.

> *Lena comes out in the clothes she wore the day she ran away from home. In this simple dress, she looks even more childish than before, but the dreamlike quality is gone. She is, simply, a frightened young girl.*

The castle and its keepers are abandoned, and in her breaking free Lena leaves behind the Nazis' evil and the dying European culture. But the playwright clearly emphasizes the need to use the hurtful or outmoded experiences of the past to accumulate the lessons that make life "worthwhile." The curtain falls at midnight—the beginning of a new day, a new life, and, a year later, a new nation: Israel.

The Workroom spans the years 1945–52, when France and its citizens were coming to terms with the new world after the German defeat. The play focuses on the conditions in a Jewish-owned tailor shop, slowly revealing the personalities and histories of its workers, primarily the six women seamstresses and their boss. The greatest attention is given to Simone, who is frustrated in her attempt to secure a pension for her family because she lacks proof of her husband's death in a concentration camp. Nonetheless, her spirit remains strong and her character uncomplaining and generous. In the last scene, Simone's young son arrives at the workroom to announce that his mother has been taken to the hospital; her recovery from an unnamed illnesss seems unlikely. Her absence is lamented, but we have no doubt the workroom will manage without her, and, in the near future, will remain functioning as a humane if contentious refuge for people who, while aiming to better their lives, seem assured of at least muddling through.

The playwrights of both *Lady* and *The Workroom* are dedicated to presenting an image of life after the Holocaust, which, though frought with difficulty and burdened by memory, possesses the human energy necessary for continuance. Both plays deal with survivors in post-Holocaust Europe and in doing so assert a theme that is formally comic in design: that despite the terror of the past, a better life is possible if we are committed to carrying on with life. Both plays are characterized by a mixed emotional tone, although Grumberg's range is much wider than Goldberg's because his play is much less philosophical, if equally discursive. *The Workroom* possesses moments of genuine delight, almost farcical in their execution; Goldberg's play is more dour, preferring to alleviate the seriousness of its argument with occasional wist-fulness rather than humor. In mood, neither play is comic or tragic, but because the action of both is directed at an open-ended future (in Israel or elsewhere), their somberness becomes a tonal antagonist to their thematic hopefulness, creating a tragicomic vision.

III

In a 1958 essay, "Experience of the Theatre," Eugene Ionesco wrote of the theatre audience's resistance to be moved and his method for overcoming this emotional recalcitrance:

> We need to be virtually bludgeoned into detachment from our daily lives, our habits and mental laziness, which conceal from us the strangeness of the world. Without a fresh virginity of the mind, without a new and healthy awareness of existential reality, there can be no theatre and no art either; the real must be in a way dislocated, before it can be reintegrated. To achieve this effect, a trick can sometimes be used: playing against the text. A serious, solemn, formal production or interpretation can be grafted onto a text that is absurd, wild and comic. On the other hand, to avoid the ridiculous sentimentality of the tear-jerker, a dramatic text can be treated as bufoonery and the tragic feeling of a play underlined by farce. Light makes shadows darker, shadows intensify light. For my part, I have never understood the difference people make between the comic and the tragic.[28]

Ionesco's description of how the comic and tragic reflect and influence each other in their themes and forms is directly applicable to Kenneth Bernard's *How We Danced While We Burned* (1973)[29] and Peter Barnes's *Laughter!* (1978).[30] The two playwrights pursue identical ar-tistic goals through similar Ionesco-like theatrical strategies. In addi-tion, both incur enormous risks in performance. The danger for Ber-nard and Barnes is that in trying to foster "healthy awareness," they create images that repel and outrage audiences to the point of total rejection.

In *How We Danced,* Bernard uses the metaphor of a cabaret to con-vey his sense of Holocaust suffering and at the same time to confront audiences for their refusal to become involved with its legacy except in the most superficial of ways. *"This play takes place in Hell,"* announces the stage direction, with a decor *"of a small overheated German beer hall."* The action inside the hall (that is, the theatre) consists of terrified "patrons" performing some kind of theatrical activity in front of an audience as a last chance to save their lives. Thus the structure of the play is essentially comic; through a parody of a bizarre quiz or talent show where only the smallest percentage of "contestants" are able to "win" the prize of postponing their deaths, Bernard describes the horrible existence endured by inmates of concentration camps. (Compared to the violence and graphic terror of this theatrical enactment of Nazi depravity and human suffering, the hell of Sartre's *No Exit* is benign and almost pleasant.)

The doomed "performers" sit *among the audience* and, when their number is called, move from their "safe" space into the theatrical arena where, under the spotlights and in front of the single door marked "Exit," they desperately try any tactic that will prolong their survival. Thus, while the "performing" is laughable in the sense of being hideously amateur for the audience watching the "show," the true context of the action (the concentration camp experience) distorts the comedy into a horrifying picture of human suffering. The historical premise of the play comes in part from the knowledge that Nazi brutality in the concentration camps occasionally was suspended or alleviated for the most whimsical or accidental of reasons.[31] In the play, if the "performers" can manage to please the "judge" of their "act"—in a way not even they can predict—they may gain a temporary reprieve from walking through the final "Exit" door upstage that leads to the waiting gas chambers.

In a performance of *How We Danced,* the "contestants" as well as the audience are harassed by the waiters and waitresses in the "beer hall" while being served food and drink, an additional aspect of the emotional disorientation that results when awful events are placed within a seemingly contradictory context. The servers are dressed like the audience but have another function in the play: they offer ugly, often bloodthirsty responses to the "contestants" and physically reinforce the authority of the cabaret's "master of ceremonies" whose deadly theatrical fancy the "performers" are trying to please.

In the Commandant (the emcee), Bernard has created an extraordinary character, by turns charming, ingratiating, vulgar, cruel, frightening, loathsome, and, in the context of his situation, immensely talented. His authority comes from his theatrical charisma as well as from his status as arbiter of the theatrical contributions of others; his repulsive and brutal decisions, which result in sentencing the "performers" to a hideous death, are partly ameliorated by the audience's recognition that they are watching an extraordinary actor at work in the part of the Commandant, a comic star in a "bad" production. Though his own performing may be crude, it is splendidly accomplished, and the level of manic energy he possesses, along with the fullness of his comic invention and the intense commitment to the horrible "part" he plays, is tremendously exciting. Once in action, the Commandant "plays against the text"; his performance creates both intense audience involvement and, simultaneously, an emotional rejection. Further, for most of the performance of How We Danced, the Commandant's own complex relationship to the stage business is undisclosed.

When the Commandant's past is finally revealed, he gives his own "performance" with an intensity that shatters any tendency to stand apart from the experiences of the Holocaust's victims, and for the moment destroys the Commandant's own objectivity about the role he is playing. The "real" audience has seen a succession of inept, bizarre, and grotesque skits, including Yiddish and German singers, Hitlerian ballet dancers, Shakespearean orators, clumsy puppeteers and boxers, plus an extended dramatic parody of a medieval romance. The sequence of "acts" all leads up to the moment when, amid great confusion as the "performers" (and perhaps some of the "real" audience too) are herded to the "Exit" door in preparation for the "late show," the Commandant explains his own agonizing situation.

> Wait! Wait! One thing I forgot. (Pause. Softly, to audience) The whole world is silent. You hear it? (In Yiddish) The world is silent! (Angrily) Listen, you don't make no accusation, huh? What I do for you, you swine, it ain't easy. Somebody, he's got to live to tell about it.—Why me? Why not? I paid for my job. Listen, I paid. My wife: dead. My children: dead. The last one, Itzik, he sees me when he gets off the train. You listen! Me, I don't have this job then. I'm carrying the clothes they take off, keeping my head down, running. You get a black eye (He draws a finger across his throat)—finished. No marks on the face, see! And you run, you die running, you don't look, you're scared all the time. (Sound track of confused people, shouts of guards, train noises) And he says, "Daddy, I've found you!" And he cries. Itzik cries. My little boy cries because he's frightened and he's found his Daddy. And me, I'm stopping my running. He's my son! My head, it's going to be smashed in. "Itzik, go wash," I say. "We'll talk later." No, no, he says, he don't want to leave me again. He's gonna lose me, he says. He's afraid. His mother—He's all alone. My Itzik is all

alone! What's happening? he asks me. Tell me, Daddy. And me, I'm not running. I'm keeping my head low in the bundle of clothes. Itzik! I scream, for God's sake, *wash first, talk later!*—And I run, I run. ([. . .] *Crying*) I run all day. All day, and still I can't sleep. He was a good boy. He went and he washed. And when he washed, when they spritzed him with . . . did he yell out—*Daddy, where are you?* I hear him! I hear him! God, I hear him! *Daddy!*—I paid! I paid! I paid!

The moment is terrifying, totally destroying the comic presumption of the performance. The play concludes with the Commandant giving instructions to the newly arriving "patrons" about the Hell he supervises; while a Bach cantata is heard, the lights fade, and "*no bows.*"

The emotional power of *How We Danced* is as great as the performance problems it raises. Can audiences sit through this kind of a play, amused and abused, sometimes at the same time? Does the initial shock of the performance wear off, only to be replaced by a refusal to "engage" the material? Is Bernard's vision of the horror of the Holocaust acceptable under the terms he presents it, that is, through a comic form that, like a monstrously extended "sick joke," must first destroy seriousness before it can be taken seriously? Can images that create a sense of physical obscenity in the audience also convey the moral obscenity of the Holocaust? The answers to these questions become clear through a performance of *How We Danced,* a most extraordinary example of the tragicomic in Holocaust drama.

Peter Barnes's *Laughter!* is a collection of two one-act plays, *Tsar* and *Auschwitz.* Each play attempts to address the issue of the place of laughter in a world filled with atrocity, and each play, for most of its length, is *written as a comedy,* filled with sight gags, one-liners, farcical business, witty reversals of identity, and a general refusal to take life or art too seriously for too long.[32] *Tsar* deals with the murderous career of Ivan the Terrible, slaughterer of hundreds of thousands in medieval Russia. *Auschwitz* takes up the theme of the Nazi genocide of the Jews, but from the perspective of ordinary German bureaucrats who, on a daily basis and with little knowledge and less concern, make the extermination of the Jews possible. Of the two plays, *Auschwitz* is the longer and the more complicated, closer to our concerns as well as to our times. (But, of course, Barnes's point is that atrocity is universal, transnational, and transhistorical.) Like Bernard's play, *Laughter!* presents a terrifying vision of human suffering and depravity comically (at first) and, along with its critical speculations on dramatic form, possesses a special place among Holocaust dramas for its emotional ferocity and intellectual provocation.

Laughter! begins with a single spotlight on *"the immaculately dressed Author,"* whose first words, "Ladies and Gentlemen," are interrupted when a hand

> slaps a large custard pie straight in his face. As he wipes it off a laughing Voice declares: It's going to be that kind of a show, folks!

The Author continues, and articulates the intellectual argument (and its antithesis) with which Barnes unifies his two plays.

> No it isn't. Gangrene has set in. Comedy itself is the enemy. Laughter only confuses and corrupts everything we try to say. It cures nothing except our consciences and so ends by making the nightmare worse. A sense of humour's no remedy for evil. . . . Laughter's the ally of tyrants. It softens our hatred. An excuse to change nothing, for nothing needs changing when it's all a joke. *(His bow tie whirls round and round; he angrily pulls it off.)* So we must try and root out comedy, strangle mirth, let the heart pump sulphuric acid, not blood. *(The carnation in his buttonhole squirts water; he tears it off desperately.)* Root it out! . . .

The phrase "Root it out!" is repeated on seven other occasions, each time as a conclusion to a serious scene that has veered off track into a kind of bizarre vaudeville. The phrase, always delivered to the audience, also serves to drive home Barnes's point that people resort to joking when in the presence of suffering, and by distancing themselves through laughter they absolve themselves of the need for concern or compassion. Barnes writes a Holocaust play that flagrantly exploits the comic form so that he can detach the serious issues from their implications, offering the audience emotional distance from the savage spectacle. But he turns the tables on the audience at the play's conclusion by refusing to provide the mechanism that will allow for detachment; in fact, he proves that what had enabled objectivity—a comic interruption or *shtik*—now reinforces the seriousness of his play. In the context of the Holocaust, and in the setting of the concentration camps, comedy *is* tragedy.

In *Laughter!,* Barnes asks whether rooting out comedy, were it possible to do so, would restore the crucial links to others in distress. He makes the inquiry using his own play to exemplify the dilemma the comic stance produces in a corrupt and inhumane world. In *Auschwitz,* the comedy temporarily locates the play in that protected realm where danger and hurt are not to be seriously considered. Most of the play is a theatrical cartoon more interested in satirizing the impersonal language and inherent corruption of large bureaucracies, German efficiency and sentimentality, ideological fanaticism, and, most pointedly, Hitler and the Nazi regime itself.

As a result of this comic strategy, we richly enjoy Barnes's three office workers, who seem to be trying to cope with the troublesome detail of everyday life, complaining humorously about food shortages and the boredom of routine labor. But what the three really discuss (among other subjects) are the Nazi killing of "undesirables" and the competitive bidding on the construction of new gas chambers for Auschwitz. Barnes uses comic language to prove his intellectual point: that the horror of atrocity *can be neutralized* if it is referred to in language detached from serious feeling, and that no institution does this to greater effect than governmental bureaucracies. A typical scene between Cranach, Else, and Stroop and their fanatical Nazi antagonist Gottleb shows the way Barnes uses the language while mocking it and then calls our attention to the joke.

> GOTTLEB *(taking out a memo):* Confirmation of this request from Brigadeführer Glucks. Memo FC/867.
> CRANACH *(showing him a memo):* Amt C operates independent of Amt D. Obergruppenführer's memo JN 72.
> GOTTLEB *(producing a second memo):* JN 72 or not. I've got a 62 KG!
> CRANACH *(flourishing a second memo):* And I've got a 17Q!
> GOTTLEB *(producing a third memo):* One 3H!
> CRANACH: Two spades.
> ELSE: Four no-trumps.
> STROOP: I pass.
> ALL: Root it out!

About two-thirds of the way through *Auschwitz,* events and people begin to turn very nasty. Gottleb forces Else and Stroop into craven betrayal of his rival, Cranach, for telling a vulgar anti-Hitler joke ("What do you call someone who sticks his finger up the Führer's arse?" "A brain surgeon"), which is continually repeated until the humor of it disappears. As with the joke, the play is slowly purged of its comedy, until it disappears entirely in Gottleb's ten-minute speech describing the murder of Jews in the concentration camps. It is a speech of such graphic terror and astonishing cruelty that the three office workers, *"twisting frantically to escape the sound of his voice,"* are made to "*gasp, cough, and scream in panic*" upon hearing it. It is a feeling the audience shares, but it is only the terrifying beginning of the violent conclusion of *Auschwitz*.

Suddenly, the office file cabinets roll away and reveal "*a vast mound of filthy, wet straw dummies; vapour; the remains of the gas still hangs about them. They spill forward to show all are painted light blue, have no faces, and numbers tatooed on their left arms.*" The intellectual idea that murder is best hidden by bureaucratic paper-shuffling gives way to one of the most ghastly visual images in Holocaust drama: as Gottleb continues his savage tirade, two "Sanitation Men," the Jewish Sonderkommando squad responsible for removing bodies from the gas chambers, pass among the straw bodies and viciously abuse them, tearing their bodies apart with iron hooks before stacking them in neat piles. Desperately, the three frightened bureaucrats strike a meaningful tableau: "*Else covers her eyes, Stroop his ears, Cranach his mouth.*" Cranach protests:

> We merely administer camps which concentrate people from all over Europe. Are we going to let the wet dreams of an obscene buffoon like Gottleb drive us out? He said it, it's all imagination, and hard facts leave nothing to the imagination. We're trained to kill imagination before it kills us. So close mind's door, shut out the light there. . . .

But Gottleb refutes his argument with the inexorable truth (one identical to Halder's): "You can't shut it out, not word play, dream play, I've been there! It's real!" The scene concludes with Cranach, Else, and Stroop marching downstage to face the audience and sing "*with increasing savagery*" the saccharine, upbeat musical-comedy anthem, "The Brotherhood of Man."[33]

Barnes, mercilessly, refuses to let the audience leave with so simple an irony, no matter how bitter. He appends an epilogue to the play, one of the most audacious passages in all Holocaust drama: violent, horrifying, and inexpressibly sad. The Announcer's voice calls on stage a vaudeville duo of two emaciated concentration camp inmates named Bimko and Bieberstein to perform their final skit before the deadly blue gas claims them.

> *A Follow Spot picks out two hollow-eyed comics,* BIMKO *and* BIEBERSTEIN *as they enter dancing. Stage Right, dressed in shapeless concentration camp, striped prison-uniforms with the yellow Star of David pinned on their threadbare tunics, wooden clogs,*

*and undertakers top hats complete with ribbon. Carrying a small
cane each, they perform a simple dance and patter routine, to the
tune of "On the Sunny Side of the Street."*

BIEBERSTEIN: Bernie Litvinoff just died.

BIMKO: Well if he had a chance to better himself.

BIEBERSTEIN: Drunk a whole bottle of varnish. Awful sight, but
a beautiful finish. Everyone knew he was dead. He didn't move
when they kicked him. He's already in the ovens.

BIMKO: Poke him up then, this is a very cold block house.

BIEBERSTEIN: They're sending his ashes to his widow. She's going to keep them in an hour-glass.

BIMKO: So she's finally getting him to work for a living.

As they dance and joke their strength fades until, at last, they succumb.
The comedy is finally rooted out with the killing of the comedians;
"they die in darkness."

The epilogue to *Auschwitz* achieves a maximum brutality because
it is written as comedy. Relentlessly, it drives home Barnes's passionate
point in *Laughter!*: that in the face of atrocity, laughter is useless and
immoral. For those fated to die, it may be a last desperate hold on their
humanity. For those who use it to distract themselves from the reality
of evil (as audiences *are asked to do* before Barnes turns the laughter
back on them), laughter itself becomes an instrument of death. There is
no better way to prove this argument than for a master comedian to use
comedy to make comedy impossible; in order to root it out, it must be
made as tragic as the human imagination can create and endure.

Four

Revisions and Reversals

A lie makes you the hangman's assistant. It betrays the victim, and this is intolerable—because you are mimicking the victim, and the most important thing you know is the innocence you share with him. So if you lie, the world stops being sane, there is no justice to condemn suffering, and no difference between guilt and innocence—and only the mad know how to live with so much despair.

—Edward Bond
Introduction to *Bingo*

I

*T*HE appearance of Jews on the stage in dramas of the Holocaust is inevitably accompanied by the presence of the Nazis with whom they are inextricably bound.[1] At one extreme, the appearance of the German oppressors is more felt than seen, implicated figures (behind whom sits a genocidal bureaucracy) whose presence and barbarity are at the visual and aural margins of stage performance. Such is the case with Charlotte Delbo's *Who Will Carry the Word?* and Goodrich and Hackett's *The Diary of Anne Frank*. At the other extreme, Nazis assume more prominent force by becoming fully conceived and actualized characters in their war against the Jews, occasionally assuming a central focus in those dramas. The Nazi doctor (modeled after Josef Mengele) in Rolf Hochhuth's *The Deputy* and Kittel in Joshua Sobol's *Ghetto* are two such characters who represent fully defined examples of the Nazi mentality and the genocidal strategy it conceived.

The middle ground between these two extremes is occupied by a vast range of dramatic characters whose unambiguous status as Nazi or Jew is less clearly established. In fact, much interest and theatrical excitement (not to say outrage) in plays of the Holocaust is generated by characters whose *actions* seem to place them in the worlds of both oppressor and oppressed. Chaim Rumkowski in Harold and Edith Lieberman's *Throne of Straw* and Jacob Gens in *Ghetto* are examples of one type of this character, Jews who display the "Nazi tendencies" of intolerance, cruelty, and betrayal. Through certain problematical and negative aspects of their personality or behavior, they are associated with the war against the Jews, all the while remaining Jews. (In a reverse situation, plays also have been written that feature "humane" Nazis, those who show traits of kindness, compassion, or remorse. The young German soldier who commits suicide in Michael Brady's *Korczak's Children* is one example. Of larger significance is Martin Engel, the sensitive, intelligent, and unapologetic protagonist of Michael Cristofer's *Black Angel*,[2] who, after many years in prison for war crimes, returns to complicate and incite the passions of the French village he has chosen to retire to.)

There is a crucial distinction to make, however, in any discussion of the many plays that involve characters with identities overlapping Jew *and* Nazi. Figures such as Rumkowski, Gens, or even the Commandant in Kenneth Bernard's *How We Danced While We Burned*, know that their position places them in a state of ethical contamination and that their actions are, in some actual way, contributing to the Germans' loathsome work, i.e., producing war materiel or, most horribly, aiding in the extermination process itself. Nonetheless, these characters possess the crucial distinguishing characteristic that disallows them from being seen as *identical* to the Nazis: an ethical awareness that lets them acknowledge—to themselves and to audiences observing them—the terrible and repugnant dilemma they are caught in. Thus, Rumkowski, Gens, Blaustain (in *Resort 76*), and Kurtzik (in Theodore Herstand's *The Emigration of Adam Kurtzik*) all understand, or come to understand, that despite their best intentions, moral purity is impossible to maintain in their degrading circumstances, and their social struggle is redefined to incorporate a more personal one of salvaging the greatest amount of ethical passion possible in the confrontation with evil. No matter how heinous their behavior or how complicitous their actions, they are never entirely "lost" in our eyes because they retain an unkillable moral consciousness.

There is also psychological as well as historical justification for the creation of characters whose deeds issue from both passionate certainty and helpless confusion: as moral individuals we are simply not what we would aspire to become. It is true that only the rarest of known individuals, in history or art, confront evil with moral purity. Still, it is their ethical effort that we attend to, despite the certainty of their failure (though it needn't be total). But there is a harmful aesthetic treatment of the Holocaust story that *exploits* the theatrical excitement found in the confrontation between goodness and evil, in a character's attempt to remain good in the face of evil. Playwrights turn to exploitation when they are less concerned with understanding the serious moral issues raised by the Holocaust and more interested in provoking theatrical excitement. In the absence of a responsible and purposeful inquiry guiding a playwright's work, the pernicious idea of the identicalness of good and evil can occur, which, in turn, can result in stage images of goodness that are made to seem their moral opposites. Whether by authorial accident or by design, this is a theatrical phenomenon that deserves critical discussion and evaluation, one that I will address at considerable length in the succeeding chapters of this book.

There are occasional examples of artists who, grappling with the problem of good and evil, have perceived a universe where foulness *is* the normative condition. Tadeusz Borowski in *This Way to the Gas, Ladies and Gentlemen* and Paul Celan in "Death Fugue" come immediately to mind, but these two artists transcended their knowledge of evil in their austere poetry and prose. As a consequence, their work is *not* exploitative of human nature but generous to it, despite the unrelieved darkness of their vision. But there are dangers in dramatizing the conditions of suffering humanity in order to create theatrical controversy, acquire notoriety, or avoid uncomfortable truths; we note this situation whenever we remain unconvinced of the artist's own belief in the ethical structures of the universe he has created. This kind of exploitation is often felt before it is understood, as when we sense that the playwright is enjoying his grim speculations more than he should.[3]

Furthermore, the best critics of Holocaust literature acknowledge the artist's risk in dealing with material of such profound mystery and brutality. Artistic problems usually result when 1) the material is not under control in tone, style, or thought (a common occurrence in all artistic endeavors), 2) when it is disingenuously engaged, or 3) when the playwright's assumptions about how the material is being received are incorrect. Concerning the last kind of "failure," Saul Friedländer exonerates George Steiner for his *The Portage to San Cristobal of A.H.* by writing how Steiner "does not *voluntarily* invert the signs concerning the Jews";[4] Sidra DeKoven Ezrahi, commenting on the Holocaust plays of Erwin Sylvanus and Peter Weiss, writes that although some see them as vehicles of expiation, "the psychological effect may, however, be exactly the opposite";[5] and Alvin Rosenfeld, discussing the fictional transformation that results in the "domestication" of Hitler, notes that this "is the case whether an author specifically intends it or not."[6] The thinking of these three critics (and others like them) is united by their concern over the discrepancy between an author's intention and the contradictory response the art object produces in its audience. To critics energized by moral passion, works that fail the moral test, even by accident, are still deserving of condemnation even if their authors are exculpated. Their negative observations are made somewhat easier to justify because problems of intentionality seldom appear by themselves but are usually accompanied by ineptitude or exploitation.[7]

Because critics like Friedländer, Ezrahi, and Rosenfeld adhere to a strongly ethical bias in their writing on the Holocaust, they are particularly sensitive to works of art in which images of good and evil are confused or, in the most extreme cases, made identical. They take for granted that the subject of the Holocaust must be approached with skill, precision, and honesty (which in themselves will not guarantee success), because the ethical issues are so complex and the burden of memory so great. Concerning the theatre and the use of characters to exemplify moral qualities (for it is in the nature of stage characters to be exemplary), the responsibility to question and judge the characters' behavior is necessary and inescapable because on stage, in performance, characters have enormous power and an immediacy that greatly influences audiences' reception of moral ideas.

Two historical events inform all discussions of Holocaust drama. First, the destruction of six million Jews and millions of others during the Second World War is an incontrovertible fact. Second, these victims were killed by the *German* nation under Hitler. The horrible deaths of millions were brought about by the passive response as well as the active, destructive participation of German citizens who still struggle with the concrete effects of the Holocaust, including a palpable sense of guilt and shame; alternatively, they refuse to accept responsibility for Hitler's "final solution," which is not an unreasonable argument for the *postwar* generation to make. It is true that, when faced with humiliation and ruthless oppression, unprecedented until that time, a small number of Jews collaborated with the Nazis and participated in terror. But the exceptions do not refute the rule. Thus, although many Holocaust plays treat the issue of collaboration and seek to understand its cause and its consequences, few dare challenge, at least directly, the unyielding facts: Germans (and others) killed millions of Jews (and others) *and not the other way around.*

Some Holocaust plays do appear, however, to subordinate the murder of the Jews to a more abstract, philosophical investigation of the mystery of human evil; in these plays Jews themselves become abstractions and their suffering emotionally remote from us. Speculating on the causes of human behavior in times of maximum threat is an entirely appropriate artistic subject about which we should be concerned only when the facts of history, i.e., the essential conditions of the Jewish genocide, are misstated or cast into doubt by an artistic strategy containing a hidden political or personal agenda. Importantly, our understanding of historical events can be distorted by losing sight of the victims whose suffering was caused by the moral dilemmas and physical torment they experienced. This manipulation of our perspective on the Holocaust is most objectionable in playwrights who equalize the responsibility for the Holocaust among its Jewish victims and Nazi victimizers.

The stylistic decision to depict "actuality on the oblique," in Ellen Schiff's wise phrase, is one way to avoid confronting historical facts and painful truths.

> The historical records on which the drama of disaster is based document man's inability to confront inhuman circumstances head-on and the consequent necessity of a mental retreat to a vista from which empirical facts are more comprehensible. The imperative to approach actuality on the oblique, to view reality insulated by one remove or more is adroitly met by a stage already conditioned by Pirandello, surrealism and German expressionism, and dominated by the absurd.[8]

To be sure, Pirandellian investigations of illusion *versus* reality, expressionist obsessions with individual psychic breakdown, or absurdist parables of existential meaninglessness are artistic forms that, in themselves, are the carriers of an infinite number of themes, serious or trivial. Individually and as a group, these twentieth-century forms have in common the tendency to reflect the fragmentation of the human personality. Because this condition opportunely coincides with the temptation to dramatize the Holocaust through personification of historical good and evil, paired characters whose identities are *interchangeable* appear in Holocaust plays of varying styles and can insulate our reality not only from "inhuman circumstances" but from clear delegation of moral responsibility.

In addition, these forms assert a presentational mode of threatrical production, where characters usually have a stage reality that calls attention to itself as a conscious invention of the playwright, and where the audience is asked to accept certain "unbelievable" premises for the action of the play. In this way too, the characters are disengaged from the "empirical facts." In the four plays that are discussed here, each playwright avails himself of a form that consciously calls attention to the stage reality of his play. All begin with mysterious, not to say bizarre, premises. And most important, all are devoted to discussions of good and evil where the protagonists' identities are fractured and their grip on reality is tenuous at best. The effect of these plays is twofold: they are exciting theatrical performances, and they confuse, rather than clarify, the central ethical distinctions about human behavior during the Holocaust.[9]

II

Stanley Eveling's *The Strange Case of Martin Richter* (1967)[10] is a political and philosophical parable (Eveling teaches philosophy at the University of Edinburgh) about the rise of fascism, the terrible effects of race and class prejudice, and the destructive power of capitalism. The play takes place in the house of an industrialist named Gümmel. During his absence the house becomes the setting for a "rehearsal" of the rise of the fascist state by Gümmel's household staff and their friends. It is a play with a deceptive simplicity, unsettling at first because we do not comprehend the premise of its (frequently comic) action and, at the end, because of the playwright's ambiguous relationship to his material. It is, however, Eveling's description of the anti-Semitic history of fascism that is most disturbing, serving as it does as a subordinate but influential component in the mixture of protofascist tendencies that tyrants and governments encourage and exploit to the point where citizens acquiesce to their own economic slavery.

The opening scene, with the "Horst Wessel Song" playing, shows us Martin Richter, Gümmel's fortyish butler, contemplating Gümmel's portrait. He speaks, as do all the characters, *"in accents which people affect as versions of a German accent";* in the adjoining room there is much commotion and cheering. Richter, although we don't know it at the time, has fabricated the identity of a fascist leader obsessed with dreams of world domination that he expresses in evocative but incomprehensible rhetoric. His followers, Gombrich (the gardener on the estate) and Hemmel (in charge of maintenance), applaud his leadership, along with the young teacher, Hans, the boyfriend of Gümmel's chambermaid, Marie. These characters represent a microcosm of society in confusion and revolt, testing its relationship to its history and to authority. The initial action of the play, in which "Leader" Richter accepts the news reports that his "National Health Party" has been victorious in the day's elections (typewriters and crowds are heard offstage), leads the audience to assume it is watching a reenactment of a postwar neo-Nazi electoral success. Only later is it clear that they have been witnessing a kind of "rehearsal for the future" enacted by a butler with a vivid imagination, a powerful voice, a strong personality, and three pathetic disciples.

Gümmel's sudden return throws his servants off guard, and Richter improvises excuses for their bizarre behavior to conceal the truth of their charade from the master of the house. When Richter's tape recording (complete with applause) accidentally reveals his plan to murder Gümmel, Richter orders his followers to "seize the criminal" and lock him up. Marie weakly protests at the end of the scene (while a traditional German folk song is heard), and as the music begins "RICHTER *and* MARIE *look up, listen and smile.*"

An undetermined amount of time elapses before the action of the next scene begins, which shows Richter in charge of the house. Marie is pregnant. The three followers construct a wooden cage and Gümmel, now a prisoner, is placed in it, whereupon he and Richter engage in a discussion of the past. We learn that "after the collapse," Gombrich and Hemmel were taken into Gümmel's service to hide their involvement in what appear to be war crimes; in return for safety and confidentiality, they agreed to their new lives of servitude. But Richter, who was already in Gümmel's employ, became jealous of the newcomers' status and angered that his own talents were unrecognized. For revenge, Richter blackmailed the others into following him, using a coercive if fraudulent strategy that contains great historical resonance.

> RICHTER: I told them that a new programme was emerging from the wreck of the old. I became the prophet of the new movement. I used to lie awake at night inventing new slogans. We acted the day we would march into power again. We gave a name to those who stood between us and authority. We called that impediment . . .
>
> GÜMMEL: Gümmel. I see. I see. But Martin. You're a Swebian.
>
> RICHTER *(Very agitated)*: Don't say that. Not even when we're alone.
>
> GÜMMEL: But you are, you are. I protected you. One word from me and you'd have been little flakes of ash fluttering on the wind. I kept it dark. You're a pure Swebian; if there can be such a thing.

RICHTER: Yes, I'm a Swebian. But what I told them was that you were a Swebian.

GÜMMEL: Richter. I'm angry. An old family like mine. Now, for the first time, I'm really angry.

RICHTER: I showed them the depth of their degradation. They were servants, bound to the service of a Swebian. From that moment they were mine.

GÜMMEL: Not for long, Martin. One word from me and they'll cut your throat from ear to ear.

RICHTER: I think not, Gümmel. I think not. They would only regard it as another Swebian lie.

(scene 2)

In this conversation, where "Swebian" and "Swebish" can be read as *Jew* or *Jewish,* Eveling introduces the racial component of Nazi fascism. At the same time, he continues the ambiguity of Richter's action, since we are not yet sure if the "new Leader" is insane or playing a game of insanity with Gümmel for real political advantage. Richter's grasp of reality will have a bearing on how we are to receive the meaning of his multiple identities. At the end of the scene, Richter speaks of the death of his father, "my old Swebish man," who was "crushed like an egg" on a riverbank by persons we assume were Nazis during the war. In the presence of his caged prisoner, and standing *"stock-still,"* he shouts "You damned Swebish man," in a way that makes us doubt Richter's sanity because only Gümmel is onstage to hear him. Still, with the insult, Richter (following the parable's structure) is calling *Gümmel* a damned Jew, by which he means a deceitful, murderous, yet feeble subhuman. Richter's game of political insurrection takes an extraordinary turn at that moment when the identities of Swebian (Jew) and non-Swebian (German/Nazi) are exchanged. Richter, now having identified himself as Swebish, abandons his weaker, humiliated self and is transformed into the charismatic, powerful image of a superior being.

The element of uncertainty about the meaning behind Richter's behavior continues in the next scene. Set in the garden, Hans and Marie enjoy the peaceful outdoors while their conversation is interrupted frequently by deep groans: the sounds of Hemmel "practicing on" Gümmel. Richter arrives, however, to show that the noise is only a tape recording. He is followed by Gombrich, who announces that Gümmel has had a seizure. When the groans begin again offstage we don't know if the sounds are artificial or "real," that is, whether or not we are hearing Gümmel die. Hemmel switches on music to drown out the groans, after which Richter leaves to "expedite his [Gümmel's] passing," and returns to declare "It was a merciful release." The scene ends, leaving us with unanswered questions: "Is Gümmel dead? Did Richter kill him? Above all, what exactly is the nature of the play's action and Eveling's relationship to it?

At dinner in scene 4, Richter is in total control, successfully getting his three disciples blind drunk. They toast the past and their future under the National Health Party, and when Gombrich asks "What was he . . . like in the early days?" Richter creates an adulatory pagan vision of the dead leader, whom we must assume is Hitler. They drink more and spew out neo-Nazi rhetoric. Hemmel describes their continuing attachment to the old "dream as sublime as our mountains," but credits its demise to "the grotesque and horrible phenomenon of Swebishness." Then, seeming to recollect his own past, he describes how he once killed an old man at a riverbank, and we conclude that it was he who killed Richter's father many years before. They descend into a drunken stupor, all except Richter, who describes his own meeting with the Leader. He speaks of "an old Swebish legend" of betrayal, and refers to the advice the Leader gave him: "The strong, he said, must never be weak. The strong are torn to pieces by the strength of weakness," which we take to be a reference to the "Swebian" threat, to the "danger" of compassion, or both.

Whatever its meaning, we are witness to the full merging of Richter's identity with the Hitlerian ideal. Richter provokes a violent argument between Gombrich and Hemmel; very drunk, they attack each other with forks. When Richter orders Hans to get a pistol and shoot the one he will identify as a traitor to their cause, we suspect that Richter is finally taking his "Swebian" revenge by arranging for them to destroy each other. Instead, Hans returns with the surprise announcement that Gümmel is alive and Richter, at last, explains the meaning behind his actions.

> RICHTER: I will tell you now, animals. It is very simple. I have an interest in your deaths. It would be a sunny and pleasant time for me when you are dead, you [Hans] Mueller, you Gombrich, you, yes, you, Hemmel. I had a deep desire for your deaths. I thought it fitting that a Swebish man should enjoy the fact of your deaths.
> GOMBRICH: Swebish. Who is Swebish? Richter? Who is Swebish?
> HEMMEL: That man, that man there, that slow, fat man. Leader

Richter. Now I recognize it clearly. I smell it. He gives off the sweet smell, the fetid odour of a Swebisher. Can you smell it, Hans? Is your nose trained like mine?
HANS: I notice the face, Herr Hemmel. That is enough.

(scene 4)

Scene 5 is a farcical chase through the garden at night, as the drunken disciples, now disenchanted with Richter, attempt to capture their former leader.

The last scene begins in darkness also. In the house, the plotters discuss their options, which include killing Gümmel and the captured Richter and sending both to "their Swebisher sky and say they killed each other." But Gümmel is in the room listening and switches on the light, whereupon the "servants" revert back to their attitudes of confusion and cowardice. Hemmel puts forward their best case ("it would be most unfortunate for you if it were ever known that you helped us to conceal ourselves, and very unfortunate for you if it were ever known in certain circles that you harbored a Swebisher in your house . . ."), and Richter, when asked to explain himself, responds strangely that "the fires have all gone out, Herr Gümmel. The smoke is in my mouth." Finally, Richter declares to his uncomprehending captors, in language only slightly less puzzling to us:

> I would like to . . . say . . . goodbye . . . to all the faces that walked past me in my nightmare, goodbye friends, goodbye Helmut, Johan, Georg, Ute, Gerda, Anna, too many names to say goodbye to, many faces that mourn past my eyes with their long dead lives wrapped round them . . . smoke has made my eyes all red . . . I can't see . . . Helmut, Anna, smoke in the sky . . . smoke in my mouth . . . in my mouth . . . the taste of smoke . . . in my mouth, Herr Gümmel . . . I see backwards . . . Whenever I look . . . I see backwards.

(scene 6)

The final moments of *Martin Richter* show the reinvesting of power and authority in the "indestructible, necessary" Gümmel. His followers all swear allegiance to him and his creed: "To him that has, more shall be given, and to him that hasn't, even what he has shall be stripped from him." One by one they all revert to their former positions of subservience. The economic and political implications of Eveling's parable stand out boldly as Gümmel, the embodiment of autocratic, capitalist, eternally victorious Germany, asserts the inescapable human attraction to economic fascism, which, it appears, can subdue and exploit all human impulses, and reconcile all human differences. He says:

> Gümmel's appetite is insatiable. Isms are nothing, divisions are nothing, hate each other, love each other, what does Gümmel care about that, he is good, wise, generous, indestructible. Gümmel the creator, Gümmel the financier, Gümmel the be all and end all. That is my name. The three names of Gümmel. . . . I see a new future for you all. For me nothing ever changes. But I see for you a new and practical future, without remorse, without sin. Each man his own form of transportation, each man his own four bed-roomed, detached residence. Well, Martin. What do you say? (RICHTER *draws out his white butler's gloves, slowly draws them on*).

The play concludes with Richter's final spasm of compassionate memory ("Helmut. Anna. Johann, Johann, Johann"), after which he leaves the stage to attend to Gümmel in his bath. His capitulation is total and, although achieved with seeming reluctance, is clearly indicative of his participation in his own exploitation. His departure is followed by an action of startling theatricality. With the stage empty and silent,

> MARIE *and* HANS *return. They bow to the audience.* HEMMEL *and* GOMBRICH *come in. They also bow. Then* GÜMMEL *and* RICHTER. GÜMMEL *takes his portrait and stands behind it)*
> GÜMMEL: All friends. Feuds forgotten.
> RICHTER: How nice everything is.
> HEMMEL: Shall we sing the evening song, Herr Gümmel?
> GÜMMEL: What a good idea. Hemmel, will you give us a chord. (HEMMEL *takes out a tuning fork and sounds it. They all test their voices.* HEMMEL *steps forward and conducts.*)
> HEMMEL: One, two, three . . . (*Song:* "GUTEN ABEND, GUT'NACHT." *They bow, smile, clap. Bow again. Go off.* CURTAIN *closes on song:* "ES KLAPPERT DIE MUHLE.")

Eveling has dramatized the story of fascism's rise and of capitalism's success, which, under the terms of his analysis, are reconcilable, inevitable, and recurring. His vision is philosophically grim, occasionally presented in highly comic action. The eternal Jewish threat described in the play is a companion to the story of how capitalism destroys everything in its path through ruthless exploitation. Richter's challenge to Gümmel is unsuccessful in part because he operates out of the past, for individual, personal motives that seem to sap his energy. Similarly, in his opposition to fascism, he is clever but fatally weakened by incapacitating memory, and he succumbs. His opposition to fascism and capitalism is neutralized. It is important to see that he is the enemy of both socioeconomic systems.

At the play's conclusion, Richter accepts Gümmel's rule and joins the others in a final satirical image of a homogenous, collective endeavor under the new regime. Together, they show the audience, *as characters,* how ineffectual they have become. Nor is there any longer a concern for Swebishness. Richter's rebellion, at first appearing to be motivated by revenge for the death of his father and his friends at the hands of war criminals, simply disappears, as if his suffering, like his "heritage" were only a pretext for keeping our attention until Eveling can finally reach the political point he was, from the first, aiming at. Alongside the larger concerns of Eveling's parable, Richter's lesser cause is very secondary, his Swebish background serving merely as a useful plot complication.

Although Richter's background merges with the identity of the oppressor's—in the cage scene and the dinner scene there is little need to play the Führer since the "opposition" contains no threat—he derives no practical benefit from the merger because his historical memory is a permanent, debilitating impediment. He can be neither political fascist nor economic capitalist. His weak Swebian resolve (as in his failure to kill Gümmel) destroys his chance to succeed in a revolution in which he has no real interest. In fact, although the playwright uses Richter's "history," he seems to have no real interest in it. Thus, the image of the Swebian Richter becoming, if only briefly, the thing he is most inclined to reject, is of theatrical interest only. Richter's "success" over his pathetic colleagues is comically advanced because Eveling prefers to avoid the serious implications of the anti-Semitism of his plot; he is not very interested in Richter or us "seeing backwards." The dead people Richter remembers as having been turned into smoke are only liabilities to him, apparently lying at the source of his crippled will, his jealous nature, his feeble self-image, and his talent for theatricals. Since the only positive characteristics he possesses are the ones that defeat him, his capitulation to Gümmel and his integration into the reinvigorated societal order are merely a postponed inevitability. He is different from his three temporary disciples only in history, not in substance; Swebish is a kind of useless incapacitating eccentricity.

We must resist, however, the idea that Swebians are either protofascists or participators in their own downfall, historically speaking. That they survived the "collapse" (with the aid of their oppressors!)

only to accept subjugation and enslavement of related kind is a morally dangerous and historically unjustified statement. Eveling works hard to distract us from these uncomfortable thoughts by employing two tactics. First, in the play's final scene, he shifts his attention to the economic factors of an invigorated fascist capitalism and away from the historical component of the story. In the end, Richter is *not* physically destroyed—in fact he appears to succeed with an enhanced status—leaving us to ponder Eveling's real theme: that all varieties of difference can be tolerated and all resistance neutralized if the structure and control of the economic system are preserved. Prejudice and genocide need not be deplored because, to the coming order, they are part of a meaningless history; in the parable's final moments, they can be passed over for the "larger" lesson.

Second, Eveling distracts us from the seriousness of the Swebish-Jewish theme by treating it in a way that seems to trivialize it. The mocking tone of much of the play seems at variance with the sense of legitimate concern Eveling shows for the terrible future he sees awaiting us. (Whether we agree with his political assessment or not is not of concern.) The drunken dinner and the garden chase are the clearest examples of an uncomfortable linkage of farce with images of economic slavery and genocide, a linkage that is both possible and effective when done well, but that is not the case here.

It is true that Eveling's considerable theatrical skill is prominently displayed in his use of unexplained or mysterious events. Eveling manipulates the audience's understanding, and the resultant confusion often effectively maintains theatrical interest, as with the groans on the tape recorder in scene 3. But the questions raised about Martin Richter's historical past, present mental condition, and future behavior are unresolved or else purposefully confused (as with the image of "fascist Swebians"). It is finally the "racial" issue that makes the case of Martin Richter so strange and distressing. Because there is no escaping the condition (demanded by the structure of the parable) which makes *Swebish* a synonym for *Jewish,* the final act of capitulation in the light of history is more problematic and difficult to accept than an imagined universal future of economic slavery. Whether fascism can flourish so easily and exploitation triumph so completely are important ideas provocatively advanced by the playwright. In its social concerns, *The Strange Case of Martin Richter* evinces genuine anxiety. It is the part of the play that deals with the final solution to the Swebian question that gives ground for disquiet and concern of a different kind.

René Kalisky's *Jim the Lionhearted* (1972)[11] is one of several plays in which he explores the issue of Jewish identity. His particular context in *Jim* is the relationship of Jews to the Holocaust, a concern that is dramatized as a surreal fantasy. Kalisky was a writer, notes one of his translators, "lacking first hand familiarity with the practical exigencies of the stage [who] was at greater liberty than other playwrights to create works for which a method of realization is yet to be devised."[12] Without the familiarity, Kalisky may have been able to give his imagination freer rein in the creation of his stage images, and it would be incorrect to see his play as anything but eminently stageworthy.

The scenic centerpiece of *Jim* is the bed in which Jim spends most of the play, in front of which is painted a giant red swastika. Around the bed congregate an assortment of Nazi leaders (Hitler, Himmler, Heydrich, Eva Braun, among others) who are the product of Jim's own unfettered imagination. The entire play, in fact, is to be seen as a hallucination within which Jim wrestles (literally and figuratively) with his attraction to the very powers that seek his annihilation. The dreamplay structure blunts the edge of Jim's obvious philonazism, but the reciprocal affection shared by Jim and Hitler remains exceedingly troublesome. In the absence of traditional narrative or linear chronology (the time of the play shifts back and forth across and beyond the entire period of the Third Reich, and the characters refuse to succumb to any sort of realistic interpretation), our attention is held by the play's hysterical energies and its bizarre and startling images.

Whatever else can be said about *Jim,* the play is a highly theatrical and highly personal statement that resists objective analysis; Kalisky's own description of it is accurate: "the writing style of the play is a continuous transformation/alternation of time and thought."[13] In addition, *Jim the Lionhearted* is held together in performance by the central visual icons of bed and swastika, and by the symbiotic relationship between Jim and his Hitlerian creation, which, in a more realistic presentation, would be impossible to believe or accept.

Jim's abused and disordered exterior is analogous to his mental condition. He is a Jewish "reject" (his name is a shortened form of Chajim), a stuttering, complaining, frightened creature whose hatred for other Jews is the result of their refusal to ignore his indolence or to provide his pension. His own anti-Semitism is in stark contrast to his fascination with and affinity for Nazi history and myth. In his mad imaginings, Jim becomes Hitler's confidant and adviser, and Hitler returns the favor by giving him considerable influence over his own personality and his racist, fawning flunkies. "You're a Jew who's scared of the misdeeds done by other Jews," says the Jew-hating Hitler, to which Jim responds with a *"cry from the heart"*: "I . . . I am a victim!" In fact, Hitler is also presented in the play as a victim of his medical and ideological advisers. He appears initially as a somewhat confused, severely drugged nonentity who is transformed under Jim's growing influence into stronger, much nastier stuff.

Jim the Lionhearted lacks neither comic invention nor theatrical surprise. What it does lack is any indication that Kalisky (whose father died at Auschwitz and who survived the war in hiding) is concerned with the Holocaust as a repository of certain historical truths. His attention is elsewhere, i.e., on the psychological debilitation of Jews after centuries of persecution and on the Jewish attraction (as he sees it) to the dark forces that oppress them. His artistic influences derive from a distinctive French tradition. Thus, although his nonrealistic theatrical methods resemble Brechtian "alienation" at times, unlike Brecht he has no political program to recommend or social message to convey.[14] Nor in his departures from realism does he reveal any of the mystical, brooding atmosphere of Strindberg. It is in Jarry and Kalisky's fellow Belgian Ghelderode, both of whom produced phantasmagorical cartoons for the stage, that we can see the artistic antecedents of Kalisky.

But Kalisky's fanciful, bizarre imagination (as when Jim does a Hasidic dance to Albinoni's *Adagio* while Heydrich plays the violin) has its perverse aspect as well. Three incidents at the play's conclusion are representative: Hitler, Jim, and Ohlendorf ("the Bard of National Socialism") forcing a cyanide capsule down Himmler's throat while Jim shouts "Sieg Heil!" (not once but three times); Eva Braun trying to seduce Jim, after which she commits suicide; and the confrontation where the two main characters extol each other in ecstatic language.

> JIM *(radiant)*: I really only came to life with the Reich and the S.S. . . . That's when my heart beats in unison with so, so many people. . . .
> HITLER *(going up to Jim)*: You've come to life, Jim, because we stirred up the embers, and you'll thrill even more and more because the time has come for the individual to be replaced by the type.
>
> (scene 9)

Despite the fantastic premises of *Jim,* we have serious misgivings about the sentiments expressed and the images created, their wild theatricality notwithstanding, because they are unattached to any moral struc-

ture. The final action, where Jim wrestles with Hitler for a pistol, trying to prevent his Führer's suicide so that he can commit his own, is the
last theatrical gesture of a disordered personality in a state of near
paralyzed self-loathing.

As we might expect with plays of this type (postexpressionism with
a French face), the meaning of scenes like those noted above is in no
way clear, if we assume they have a meaning at all. Except in a kind of
weightless, abstract way noted by David Willinger ("here [are] Hitler
and Jim together in a faceoff on the stage of history, locked in a mortal
combat that has no resolution"[15]), *Jim the Lionhearted* is fainthearted
and fuzzy-headed despite its theatrical invention. There is a cruel irony
in the play's title, which points to its wonderful kind of irresponsibility,
where the marvelous theatricality of the playwright transposes the
reality of the Holocaust into the mind of a Jew-hating, Nazi-loving
clown hallucinating on the bed of history.

The emotional reaction that greeted Robert Shaw's *The Man in the
Glass Booth* (1967)[16] was a sure indication that the play's provocative
imagery and thematic ambiguity would not be taken lightly by theatre
audiences. The *New York Times*'s two critics, Clive Barnes and Walter
Kerr, while praising the play's theatricality, expressed considerable
concern over its lack of clear ideas, a feature of the 1967 London production that was preserved when the play moved to Broadway the next
year.[17] A close reading of the text gives later critics cause for continued
uneasiness about its meaning. Like the other plays discussed in this
chapter, *The Man in the Glass Booth* derives its power to disturb from
its peculiar perspective on Holocaust history as revealed through the
dramatization of one man's Jewish identity crisis. There is even a temptation not to take the play seriously because Shaw, a splendid and ac-
claimed actor, is so flagrant in his use of melodramatic incident and
purposeful obscurity, as the play's first scene shows.

Arthur Goldman, Shaw's multimillionaire protagonist, is first seen
in his luxurious Manhattan apartment, *"praying beside a tomb."*
Special attention is called to a locked door, a roof garden full of
statuary and artificial flowers, a priceless painting set on an easel, and a
glass elevator. Verdi's *Requiem* is heard. In the next few minutes,
Goldman shows an unaccountable suspicion or disdain for everyone
(except toward his disciple, Charlie), lapses into speaking German,
and carries around a pistol. These objects and incidents are designed to
create a sense of mystery and expectation in the audience, an effect
splendidly achieved. In fact, all of the action of the first act is specifically devoted to keeping two questions uppermost in the audience's at-

tention: who is Arthur Goldman? and why does he behave the way he does? Thus, as the first scene ends, Goldman *"holds up the cigar, draws deeply on it, and holds the lighted end under his left armpit."* The action is both bizarre and inexplicable, provoking consternation and wonder. This bit of stage business, together with others equally theatrical, makes the performance aspect of the play sheer wizardry.

But, of course, *The Man in the Glass Booth* does not (and did not) exist in a cultural-historical vacuum. Most audiences of that time would have understood that Goldman, especially in his second-act imprisonment and public trial in Israel, is a reflection of Adolf Eichmann, the Nazi officer in charge of the destruction of the Jews, who was kidnapped by Israeli agents and tried in Jerusalem during the last nine months of 1961. (He was hanged in May of the next year.) Explicit reference to the Eichmann kidnapping and trial is made in the first act of the play, which is set in 1964. What audiences might not have understood was the purpose in having the Nazi Eichmann reincarnated into the image of the Jew Goldman. Still, under the right circumstances (which Shaw supplies), they could be led to invest the time and attention necessary to reach that understanding. So it is not for nothing that Goldman, early in the first scene, makes the first of many references to the confusion of identity between Germans and Jews, since the issue is one of Shaw's central themes and part of his method to engage our interest.

> GOLDMAN: In Israel they can't even define it. J . . . E . . . W. Can't define that word in Israel. They got councils workin' at it: boards and councils. (*To* CHARLIE.) Identifying him [the man coming up in the elevator]. We're all Germans, Charlie. All Germans and all J . . . E . . . W's. So identify him.
>
> (act 1, scene 1)

The second act of *The Man in the Glass Booth,* set in the Israeli prison where Goldman has been taken, begins with a question that will be raised repeatedly in the play and with an increasing urgency. "Why did you pretend to be Jewish?" asks Mrs. Rosen, Goldman's chief interrogator, who serves as the audience's surrogate in its attempt to dispel the confusion. Convinced that Goldman is really Adolf Karl Dorff, an SS colonel who slaughtered Jews in concentration camps, she is angry over his masquerade: a Nazi playing a Jew. Goldman explains, in a purposely evasive way, that in fact he *is* Jewish, or partly Jewish: the cousin of an elderly Jewish businessman in New York named Hymie Goldman who took him in after the war and gave him a new start. But, having made this confession, Goldman launches into a horrifying description of his work as a human butcher and of the satisfaction he took in his work.

> Am I Jewish? They lay on top of their dead or dying and we shot, shot, shot. I never missed one. So the last lot lay on the pyre so high we reached up from the sides and give it [sic] at arm's length. Just a day in my life. Just a clear day to enjoy forever. Am I Jewish? I don't know about my mother, but my father was pure-blood Aryan. That I'm proud of. (*He laughs and laughs.*)
> (act 2, scene 1)

The laughter at the end of the speech provides a continually lunatic punctuation to Goldman's description of his murderous exploits. Here and elsewhere, it augments the sense of terror and increases the evidence of his mental instability. At the play's conclusion he is completely mad, that is, without any coherent identity at all.

At the trial in the last scene of the play, Goldman (now Dorff dressed in an SS uniform) is given the opportunity to "come clean." Certainly the audience expects some clarification of the situation, if not explicit answers to the "mysteries" of plot and idea that it has witnessed. In other words, all the earlier uncertainties, so carefully planned, can be understood if we can have answered the unresolved questions about the protagonist's identity. What audiences are offered instead are many clues that lead to greater obscurity of character and a fuller discussion of what really tantalizes Shaw: the related subjects of Jewish "chosenness" and survival.

The play began on Goldman's birthday, November 20, 1964, the same day as Pope Paul VI's declaration absolving the Jews of deicide. Goldman makes much fun of the two events, and their conjunction raises the issue of "chosenness" as it affects the Jews through history. Goldman says that the Jews were marked for extermination and, in their passive behavior in the concentration camps, they helped to facilitate their own destruction: "the chosen, was chosen, and well they chose!" Later, in the last minutes of the play, a mad, grinning Goldman inexplicably turns *to the audience* (unacknowledged until that moment) and says: "I chose ya because I know ya. I chose ya because you're smart. I chose ya because you're Jewish. I chose ya because you're the chosen. I chose ya for remembrance." It is left to the Old Woman, whose earlier testimony destroyed Goldman's outrageous masquerade, to respond "*desperately*": "You chose us because you love us."

The subject of survival is raised less explicitly in the play but always appears in Goldman's obsession with what he sees as the Jews' passivity in the face of Nazi brutality. His preoccupation with the issue is heard in the lyrics of his little "requiem" song in act one (*"what bells will ring for those who died/like sheep?"*) and in his other references to Jewish victims like "Mrs. Levi and her dead friends [who] got on the train in the first place." The two questions of chosenness and survival are explicitly joined at a crucial moment when Goldman concludes a long and passionate hymn to Hitler and Hitler's murderous deeds. Facing the court, he proclaims:

> People of Israel, we never denied him. And those who tell you different . . . lie. Those who tell you anything else lie in their hearts. And if, if he were able to rise from the dead, he would prove it to you now. All over again. If only . . . if only we had someone to rise to . . . throw out our arms to . . . love . . . and stamp our feet for. Someone . . . someone to lead. (*Pause. Then calculatedly.*) People of Israel . . . people of Israel. If he had chosen you . . . if he had chosen *you* . . . *you* also would have followed where he led.
>
> (act 2, scene 2)

So, at last, we perceive what is on Shaw's mind: the calculated condemnation of Jewish "superiority."[18]

In response, the Old Woman sitting *"in front of the audience rises and speaks quietly."* She explains that the man in the dock is a German Jew named Arthur Goldman, a cousin of Adolf Dorff, a Nazi concentration camp officer. Goldman's family was killed by the Nazis in the camp where both men spent the war. She describes how her fellow camp inmates "tore him [Dorff] to pieces" after the Russians liberated them—but without Goldman's participation. And, finally, she tentatively refutes Goldman's accusation: "I do not think we would have followed where the Fuehrer led." Shaw closes the play with a final powerful image: Goldman, naked inside the glass booth, the consummate human specimen (Jew and Nazi, victim and victimizer), locked in an impenetrable silence.

The silence, however, cannot distract us from questions small and large. In the former category, for example, we never do learn the identity of the flower delivery man who Goldman says is his cousin, or why Goldman is praying in the first scene. In the latter category, we never learn why Goldman has taken on Dorff's identity, although Shaw advances many suggestions for his behavior: Goldman's camp experience has left him genuinely crazy; Goldman has a Christ/martyr complex (alluded to several times in the play, most clearly in the Old Woman's accusation) and needs to sacrifice himself to exorcise the burden of his guilt for his special camp "status" as Dorff's cousin; Goldman needs to make the Nazis' case publicly, extolling Hitler and his policies in open court as an expression of feelings Germans won't reveal and/or as a way to serve "justice"; Goldman becomes Dorff so that Dorff can be brought to trial "posthumously," after which Goldman can repent for his cousin; Goldman becomes Dorff out of shame for the Jews' passive behavior and/or for his own accidental involvement in some of their deaths. In sum, there is no answer provided to the puzzle of Goldman-Dorff, only contradictory possibilities that can be spread out under the auspices of an all-encompassing, ambiguous identity. That the character provides "great theatre" is small consolation.

Shaw here is playing a game with his audience, and although he plays it superbly, he plays it less than honestly. As a playwright, he creates a pattern of unexplained incident and motivation, exploiting the audience's natural curiosity for information by providing much of it not (or not only) to "throw them off" but to conceal the fact that he has not come to any meaningful conclusion about the momentous issues he discusses. His posture, however, in the face of the mystery of human behavior, is not humility but arrogance. Shaw seems quite satisfied to distract us from the ultimate moral questions of guilt and responsibility, cowardice and bravery, good and evil, with deliberate ambiguities or confusions; that is, he is more interested in providing entertainment than clarity, titilation than confrontation, which is why he touches (in the ranting of a "Nazi") upon the inflammatory issues of Jewish "passivity" and "collaboration." From a performance standpoint, he does the job well.

In itself, providing entertainment is an entirely worthy objective, but in the Holocaust context it is inappropriate and even dangerous if it succeeds at the expense of the other, deeper concerns I have mentioned. To achieve its effects, the play relies on the exploitation of real historical suffering as well as genuine frustration over our inability to understand the reasons for it. Shaw energizes his writing by placing at the play's center the astonishing image of Jew as Nazi as Jew. His protagonist moves between both personalities because, after all, as he has told us, even the Israelis cannot agree upon the truth about Jewish identity. In sum, the knowledge that some Germans were good Jews and some Jews were bad Germans is not a license to obscure historical truth. In *The Man in the Glass Booth,* the purposeful maintenance of thematic confusion has become more attractive and important than the resolution of the play's moral tension.

Among the most recent and controversial examples of how writers use the transference of identities between German and Jew is Christopher Hampton's play, *George Steiner's The Portage to San Cristobal of A.H.*, carefully adapted from George Steiner's short novel.[19] In fact, the vociferous critical reaction to *Portage,* play and novel, was highly polarized, and re-ignited the simmering debate over how the Holocaust experience should best be approached through art.[20] Steiner, as noted in chapter 2, has made the Holocaust one focus of his lifelong critical examination of Western philosophical and imaginative literature. In his novel, and in Hampton's stage adaptation of it, we see the attempts to transform abstract ideas, many found in Steiner's book of essays *In Bluebeard's Castle,* into more popular aesthetic forms. (Because the ideas are Steiner's, and the adaptation so faithful to his prose intentions, I will refer to the play as Steiner's rather than Hampton's without meaning to detract from the latter's skilled work.)

The "A.H." of Steiner's title is Adolf Hitler, who, at age 90, has been located by a team of Israelis in a South American jungle. The five searchers are perfunctorily described by Steiner as coming from different backgrounds of belief and commitment, and each has a different reason for making the pilgrimage to retrieve the archcriminal of modern history. The organizer of the rescue party is Lieber, survivor of the Holocaust, who appears apart from the stage action, keeping in contact with the searchers through erratic, clandestine radio transmissions. Lieber seems to be Steiner's representative of all Holocaust victims who survived the horrors of the Nazis: old, passionate, obsessed, often misunderstood. More abstractly, Lieber also represents vengeance and, by implication, the God of the Old Testament. Through the play he announces the list of Nazi atrocities, remembering (for the audience's benefit too) the circumstances of the deaths of millions of murdered Jews.

> I want you to remember
> Tell me you remember
> The garden in Salonika where Mordechai
>   Zathsmar, the cantor's youngest son, ate
>   excrement
> The Hoofstraat in Arnheim where they took
>   Leah Burstein and made her watch while
>   her father
> The two lime trees where the road to
>   Montrouge turns south on which they hung
>   the meat hooks and

The pantry on the third floor, Nowy Swiat
eleven, where Jakov Kaplan, author of
"The History of Algebraic Thought in
Eastern Europe 1280–1655" had to dance
on the body of
The Mauerallee in Hanover, where three
louts drifting home from an SS
recruitment spree came across Rahel
Nadelmann, tied her legs and with a
truncheon
The latrine in the police station in
Wörgel which Doktor Ruth Levin and her
niece had to clean with their hair.

(scene 5)

A.H. is Lieber's antagonist, the representative of German criminal-
ity, the image of charismatic evil and, by implication, Satan. Their battle throughout the play concludes with an extended speech by Hitler,
who, until the final moments when he is put "on trial" in the jungle and
is roused to his own defense, has spoken only five words. His "aria" accuses the Jews of causing their own misfortune, declares the State of
Israel to be a result of the Holocaust, suggests that Hitler may have
been of Jewish ancestry, and proposes that he was, in fact, the second
messiah.

> Perhaps I *am* the Messiah, the true Messiah, the new Sabbatai,
> whose infamous deeds were allowed by God in order to bring his
> people home. "The Holocaust was the necessary mystery before
> Israel could come into its strength." It wasn't I who said that, but
> your own visionaries, your unravellers of God's meaning on a Fri-
> day night in Jerusalem. Should you not honour me? Who have
> made you into men of war, who have made of the long, vacuous
> daydream of Zion a reality? Should you not be a comfort to my
> old age?
>
> (scene 18)

It is this long monologue, quoted in part above, that has received
the most hostile response from Steiner's critics, especially because the
dubious points it makes so brilliantly are given no refutation in the
play. (Goldman's similar argument in *The Man in the Glass Booth* is
given a half-hearted refutation.) Several commentators have pointed
out the flawed theological and historical premises of the speech, and

were angered by the opportunity Steiner provided for such statements to be misinterpreted by audiences. Essentially, Steiner's critics argue that, without rebuttal, the speech contributes to the anti-Semitic environment Steiner deplores, and that it distracts from the real work of education necessary to relieve the world of its inherent racism. A typical comment is Hyam Maccoby's: "We are bound to conclude that he has aimed at a stunning near-apocalyptic effect, and it has entirely failed to come off; or in so far as it is striking, influential and effective, it was the opposite to what was intended."[21] It is another example of a playwright defeated by his own best intentions.

Steiner himself responded to the criticism, defending his work for its historical truth and moral concern. But he seemed to base his defense most firmly on empirical grounds, on the effect the play has on audiences, which he describes as intellectually stimulating and emotionally devastating. He refers in an interview in the London *Times* to "audiences [who] hold their breath and weep" during Lieber's "litany of the Holocaust."

> The answers to "A.H." *must* come from the audience, from the readers, from each and every one whose moral being is implicated in the continuing bestialities of the twentieth century. . . . To answer *for* one's reader or audience would be to break this pact [of generosity].[22]

Steiner's self-defense rests largely on his claim that a play's value lies in its ability to move audiences, but it is a slippery argument at best. Immediate responses (and some to *Portage* were distinctly negative) are not the best test of a play's value or values, and in Steiner's own case, they ignore the moral judgments of art with which Steiner has long tried to inform his own criticism. This seeming contradiction deserves attention.

Steiner is seeking, and has always sought, some answer to the question of why so culturally advanced a country as Germany could have made genocide a national policy, and then carried out that policy with so little inner restraint. The appearance of *evil from out of goodness* has provoked him to consider that both qualities *spring from the same source.* In the play, Steiner works out this idea in linguistic and thematic terms, most particularly in opposing the force of speech with the power of silence. He advances the speculation, part legend, part theological musing, that an error in transcribing the divine word was the cause of permanent and irrevocable evil appearing in the world. The idea, though quaint, is no more preposterous than Hitler being alive and well in a South American jungle. He concludes that because goodness and evil are mutually dependent and sustaining, evidence of one without the appearance of the other is impossible.

Thus, Lieber cannot exist without A.H. (he is Lieber's all-consuming obsession), and the reverse is also true. In a modern world so advanced in its cruelty, *both* Lieber *and* A.H. are survivors moving through and around in their hearts of darkness. In dramatizing how the searchers become physically weaker as they approach civilization while their captive grows stronger (an exciting aspect of the stage performance), we see manifested a belief that goodness will find its own corruption once it tries to destroy the evil upon which its existence depends. In keeping with this belief, evil assumes the attributes of goodness, allowing Hitler the astonishing declaration, "The Reich begat Israel."

Steiner seeks to show the natural attraction we have to evil and our confusion when we recognize it in ourselves. He depicts the difficulty we have in opposing evil because it is *within* us, part of us. (Lieber wants A.H. "because he is ours.") Steiner is well aware of the acts of goodness performed during the Holocaust but prefers to reflect more upon the terrible foulness that minimizes our appreciation of those actions, to show instead how ethical impurity is the true human condition. Always a rationalist, Steiner is searching to make sense of the most irrational chapter of modern history, and he resolves his confusion by proposing the idea that goodness and evil are mirror images of each other. Accepting the latter, he can, at the same time, validate the former.

At the conclusion of the play, we are presented with a single, exciting image of great resonance. As Hitler again lapses into silence ("These are my last words"), we hear the approach of helicopters over the jungle clearing. Everyone looks skyward for this most modern *deus ex machina,* trying to discern in the heavens the agent of their rescue. But there is, as yet, nothing to see, and the mechanical God only appears in the biblical way as "*the stage is raked by a fierce wind*" and, we assume, by a cloud of dust. (Earlier, one of the searchers asked: "Why haven't we seen Lieber's face?") What our eyes *do* see is Hitler on his *throne,* looking at the audience, the focus of the stage picture. While the others look elsewhere for an ambiguous deliverance, we see the face of evil, open and up close. That is where and how Steiner's search ends, for then comes the "blackout." Darkness once again descends over the world.

Steiner is acknowledging that in the confrontation with the "darkness he carries" he finds both the evil done *to* his people and the evil *in* his people. *Portage* presents an artistic vision to protect against confusion and despair by establishing a *modus vivendi* between the eternal moral opposites. It is a vision that has deep roots and that contains a fearful admission, which helps to explain Steiner's quite irrelevant appeal to the spontaneous judgments of audiences: it is an admission of either defeat or exhaustion in his personal search for untainted images of humane possibility.

George Steiner's quest seeks to understand the mystery of evil; goodness seems to require no understanding. The power of evil is at the center of the play, in its themes and strongest images. The structure of *Portage*, in fact, is like a miniature Nuremberg rally, i.e., the extraordinarily protracted and episodic theatrics leading to the appearance of the "great man" himself, who has been concealed for so long, but who is finally revealed as being among us all the time. (In this view, the play *must* end with Hitler's mesmerizing verbal performance; nobody cares about what happens after the star's work is done.) The quest, as I have noted elsewhere,[23] has a personal dimension, one that finds Steiner linking the murder of six million Jews to the discovery of his own Jewish identity. In order to relieve the discomfort of this connection, Steiner (with Hampton's assistance) has concluded his play in a way that astonishes *by its lack of a conclusion*. It is, at the end, less important that Hitler's preposterous, extraordinary diatribe goes unrefuted than it is that we are left with the idea that deliverance cannot be found in Israel—even if Hitler can be safely returned there.

In "A Kind of Survivor," Steiner argues for his place in the diaspora, making the point that Jews are a people "not in place but in time." Israel, to Steiner, is "a sad miracle." In his view, the source of the Jews' historical continuity lies elsewhere than in a "nation-state bristling with arms." *Portage* ends before we learn which country "gets" Hitler. According to Steiner, it would be a double mistake to assume that something positive would be derived from his return to Jerusalem, first, because Israel's revenge is self-destructive (the searchers weaken and falter), and, second, because Hitler, the evil we carry in us, already has an Israeli address. But there is a third reason to question the wisdom of the Jews' search for Hitler, heard in the terrible irony of Hitler's final speech, in his claim to being the Messiah-Founder of the State. "Probably the most important message that Judiasm has to bring to our time," writes Olivier Renault D'Allones, "and the most tragic explanation of the persecutions to which it is subjected, is that a culture—or cultures—need not be state controlled, or linked to a power."[24] This idea is the philosophical and political foundation of Steiner's controversial image of good and evil.

George Steiner's The Portage to San Cristobal of A.H. provides a vision of the world rooted in great and continuing battle. The air of the survivor's continual portage holds a double darkness: Job's suffering and Cain's mark. Steiner's critics have pointed out the disturbances and falsehoods of A.H.'s unrefuted rhetoric and have struck deeply at the play's credibility while confessing that the play's theatrical attractiveness is great. Yet, *Portage* proposes to find an answer to profound and troubling questions. Approving pessimists will say that Steiner looked into evil and found himself. Disappointed optimists will say that he looked into goodness and could find little of himself. Understanding realists can say that he looked into the Holocaust and found only impenetrable, inescapable mystery. Of the plays discussed in this chapter, his is the one where the ambiguity is earned and the search for understanding genuinely rewarded.

Five

Some German Voices

There are values that supersede aesthetic ones and situations in which it is unseemly to continue going through the paces of aesthetic judgment.

—Irving Howe

THE subject of the Holocaust in German-language drama is an issue of enormous complexity. Since the end of the war, German-language drama has developed in ways that exemplify the most adventurous experiments in the world of theatre production, while at the same time, as we would expect, revealing the deepest concerns of the German culture. In the introduction to *The Theatre of the Holocaust,* I referred to the playwright's dilemma concerning the dramatizing of the Holocaust experience: "how to give stage images their full burden of meaning without making them unrecognizable through abstraction or untruthful through replication."[1] In this chapter, I will explore the question of images of Jews in German-speaking drama in six plays that span several generations. All of them represent *die Bewältigung der Vergangenheit,* the overcoming of the past, which has so special a meaning for German-speaking playwrights and audiences, and all of them, in chronological order, point to the increasing abstraction of images of Jews that contributes to a troubling, if not dire, sense about the future. Anat Feinberg, in her excellent survey of the Jewish experience in postwar Austrian drama, summarizes:

A version of this essay was presented at the German Studies Association Conference, Albuquerque, New Mexico, September 27, 1986.

Contemporary Austrian drama consists of plays which barely show a trace of an attempt to account for the ills of the war years. The Jewish experience appears, if at all, as a minor theme. The historical fate of the Jews is blurred and becomes a vehicle for other thematic objectives or constitutes a metaphor for the fate of any outsider or victim in bourgeois society.[2]

Despite the concern of these six playwrights with the subject of Germans and Jews, none of the six plays discussed here has a Jewish protagonist in the usual sense, and most go out of their way to disguise the presence of Jews in the functions of the societies they dramatically describe. It is mostly through secondary characters and the comments about Jews in the texts of these plays that audiences receive the images of Jews that these German-language playwrights create. By investigating these images, we have one way of assessing the social and psychological position of Jews in society and how that position has changed in the course of several generations of mutual tension and frequent, reciprocal mistrust. Whatever else can be said about Germany and the Jews, one conclusion is inevitable: the relationship is fraught with ambivalence, contradiction, and discomfort.

I

Erwin Sylvanus's *Dr. Korczak and the Children*[3] is the earliest of the plays under discussion and, perhaps because it was written closest to the end of the war, represents an unusually humane and positive picture of Jews. *Dr. Korczak* is a one-act play using a Pirandellian dramatic form: the performers call attention to the fact that they are at work in the theatre and frequently discuss the business of role playing with the audience and with each other during the course of the performance. This device is used to test the aesthetic boundaries of the theatre itself, putting the art of the theatre under equal scrutiny with the primary story the performance is dedicated to telling.

One of three stories in *Dr. Korczak* imagines the events that led up to the deportation for extermination of Janusz Korczak, director of a Warsaw orphanage, and the children in his care. When, in 1942, Korczak—an eminent Jewish educator and social activist—was ordered to gather "his children" for transportation to Auschwitz, he chose to accompany them rather than desert them, although it was said that the Nazis had promised him his freedom if he would cooperate in making the deportation go smoothly. Today, Korczak is generally seen as one of the true heroes of the Holocaust.

The power of Sylvanus's play is surprisingly great considering the emotional disruptions demanded by its structure, and despite its narrative and scenic austerity. *Dr. Korczak* is an example of less meaning more, aesthetically speaking, and of how humane ethical conviction, movingly portrayed, can neutralize the negative effect of theatrical cliché and theological abstraction. Like all of the playwrights discussed here, Sylvanus is attacking the complacency, intolerance, and self-deception of the postwar German citizen. One of the play's English translators remarks:

> . . . *Dr. Korczak and the Children* was not written in direct reaction to the horrors of war . . . but in direct reaction to something else which . . . seemed perhaps even more morally appalling: the fantastic ease and rapidity with which the horrors had been forgotten.[4]

Nonetheless, Sylvanus avoids succumbing to despair or fatalism and chooses a more optimistic ending to his moving story by relying on the positive images of Jews who are caught up in theatrical and historical conflicts.

Along with Korczak's story, Sylvanus relates two others: that of the German soldier who delivers the evacuation order, and of the actors who are reluctantly performing the other two stories. Through this theatrical "frame" we are continually reminded that the actors are neither Jews by religion nor Nazis by choice. But the focus of the play as a whole is a historical event whose Jewish nature cannot be disguised, although it can be subordinated in its relationship with the other stories Sylvanus has to tell. The concluding scene is almost entirely comprised of the prophetic words of the biblical Ezekiel.

There is no mistaking Sylvanus's play for a piece of documentary theatre of the kind that his fellow playwrights Weiss and Kipphardt were to later excel in writing, since his historical materials are clearly "fictions" in their details and in the dramatic form through which they are presented. The strength of the play lies in its ability to engage our emotional interest in the "inner" stories of Korczak and his Nazi antagonist. The opening stage direction: *"The author has not invented the events depicted in the play; he has merely recorded them,"* like the central theme of the play, involves a lie, i.e., the traditional notion that art often lies to us in order to tell a greater truth. This aesthetic fact is connected to a historical incident concerning the imagined life of a

Jewish man who, when confronted with the most horrible dilemma, broke his personal oath never to lie in order to achieve a higher good. Sylvanus, who has "promised" not to lie to us, is, of course, breaking his oath to the audience in his care. The result is history written with a "greater" objective in mind than fidelity to fact: creating through stage images ("lies" continually and dynamically asserted) a universal story about the meaning of lies and truth.[5]

Early in the play, Sylvanus creates the image of Korczak as a boy, learning the lesson that will determine his behavior for the rest of his life. For many weeks, the young Korczak has struggled to save enough money to redeem his father's gold watch, which his mother has pawned to buy food for their family. On the day he sets out to claim the watch, he learns that it has been purchased by someone else. In despair, he turns to a rabbi for advice:

> SECOND ACTOR: I found him preoccupied, contemplating the Scriptures, which were open before him. He barely looked up, but he listened to me. He listened closely. He answered me and said, "So—you want your father's little gold watch . . . Here, take my watch. Take it. It belonged to my father." "But now you don't have a watch yourself any more, Rabbi," I said. He became very angry at that and threw me out. I went back to him, though—I went back many times, for I understood why he had been so angry and I wanted him to forgive me . . . I had a golden watch again now. It wasn't my father's watch—and yet in a sense it was our father's watch. It wasn't a cheap watch. It was the watch of a devout man who obeyed the holy laws. He was quite fond of it, probably—even a Jew is fond of things, but at that moment he had to part with it. (*He looks at the watch again.*) Otherwise he would have had to lie. Otherwise he would have had to lie to me; and a man who knows God does not lie. That's why he had to be angry . . . I made up my mind then and there to take the rabbi as a model for my future conduct: never to become angry at human weakness, only at those who would force me to lie. And I have stuck to that code.
>
> (scene 3)

(Actually, the reason for the rabbi's response remains rather opaque, and several suggestions are plausible as to why he felt tempted not to tell the truth, for example, that his watch couldn't make restitution for the one lost, that he is helpless in the face of Nazi cruelty, that he didn't want to part with it but didn't want his gesture questioned or rejected.)

Later, in scene 16, the great confrontation between Korczak's "lie" and the Nazi "lie" occurs. Actor #1 playing the SS soldier and Actor #2 playing Korczak *face the audience,* then each other, and, using identical words, declare the eternal opposition of their worlds. "I am ready," they say, one to kill and the other to be killed. The Narrator says:

> And time runs out minute by minute, indifferent as the ticking of the clock. But there is another time, a time that does not run out minute by minute, indifferent as the ticking of the clock—and that is real time, Janusz Korczak already lives in this other kind of time.

Janusz Korczak, dead in history, lives in memory and in the theatre. "I will lie—and yet I will not lie," Korczak says to the Nazi. "You, Major, of course are incapable of understanding me." Thus, Sylvanus drives home his point about his contemporary audience's willful refusal to explore its recent history and presents a clear rebuke to the Nazi mentality and system.

In the final scene, the Narrator extends the biblical allusions often heard in the play and, assuming one last role of an old rabbi, retells Ezekiel's prophecy of the resurrection of the dry bones. As the rabbi, the Narrator announces his belief in a positive future for the Jewish people. Through metaphorical language, he predicts its salvation and continuance. His reference, in the postwar context of the performance, can only be to the State of Israel, created in 1948, a political reality and an international event directly related to Germany's destruction of six million Jews. *Dr. Korczak* concludes with the image of the eternal Jew who, despite persecution across centuries, retains his humanity and inexhaustibility in the prophetic, political, and theatrical levels of the play. Korczak's murdered children (represented on stage by one boy actor) *do* survive, through metaphor in German drama, in reality in Israel.

The story of Korczak's life-affirming lie, which Sylvanus retells in the theatre, contains multiple meanings. First, it is intended as a refutation and contrast to the life-destroying lies about the Jews that produced the "final solution." Second, it contradicts the individual lies of postwar German citizens concerning their complicity in the Holocaust. Third, its performance, constantly interrupted by the actors in order to call attention to themselves and to the theatre they are working in, stresses the "lie" on which the truth of the theatre is based. *Dr. Korczak* is impressive as a highly philosophical play whose intellectual concerns are shrewdly developed and whose humane attitudes are emphatically expressed.

But it is the form of *Korczak* that is most provocative. It allows Sylvanus to assert the dignity and value of the destroyed Jewish world of Europe, while at the same time abstracting the images of that world through his use of the Pirandellian frame. Thus, Jewish images, sweet and sad, noble and melancholy, asserting life and carrying death, become doubly removed from us, absent through historical events and distant because of theatrical contrivance. But in calling attention to the form of the performance, by the end of the play, Korczak himself, as well as Jewry, becomes an abstraction. It is precisely this *loss of reality* of Jewish characters and Jewish experience, glimpsed here in the work of a concerned and humane playwright, that creates problems in the German-language drama in the years after *Dr. Korczak*.

The premiere of Rolf Hochhuth's *The Deputy* in 1963 caused, in Eric Bentley's words, "*almost certainly the largest storm ever raised in the whole history of the drama.*"[6] Ostensibly, the controversy was the result of Hochhuth's protracted, heavy-handed effort to dramatize Pope Pius XII's refusal to speak out against the Nazi persecution of the Jews during the Holocaust. The play, and the historical essay appended to it, is a sprawling and emotionally charged statement about institutional and individual cowardice concealed behind the twin masks of political hypocrisy and religious ceremony. *The Deputy* is also a play about courage and human suffering revealed in the two main characters' search for truth and justice; importantly, neither of these two characters is Jewish.

The Deputy's five acts, written in varying styles by the playwright, reveal in numerous ways how, in moments of deep crisis, evading moral responsibility for our endangered fellow human beings is both impermissable and sinful. The main carrier of this message is a young priest named Riccardo Fontana, whose intellect and family connections have made him a favorite of the Pope. His character, Hochhuth tells us in the stage directions to the play, is modeled after two courageous Christians: Father Maximillian Kolbe, murdered in Auschwitz, and Provost Lichtenberg of the Berlin Cathedral, who, early in the war, spoke out in support of the Jews of Germany and who was severely punished for his compassion and concern. Father Fontana is obsessed with righteousness, and he is moved to jeopardize his career and his life in order to save the threatened Jews of Italy. In the play's final act, set in Auschwitz, Riccardo engages in a philosophical debate with the SS Doctor, a loathsome if charismatic figure modeled after Josef Mengele, and is shot to death as he attempts to destroy the antagonist described as "this uncanny visitant from an alien world."[7]

The story of Father Fontana's travail and murder has been called by Walter Kaufmann "a modern Christian tragedy—perhaps the only Christian tragedy."[8] Kaufmann admires *The Deputy* because he is drawn to the young priest's struggle "to become a Christian in the most demanding sense of the word."[9] In other words, in the theatre, Riccardo is intended to become *our* moral deputy through his active search for goodness. Riccardo's relentless insistence on idealized Christian action is excessive, but such is the way of martyrs, both fictional and historical. The conclusion that Hochhuth draws from the life and death of his protagonist is full of significance for his audience: to be silent in the face of inhumanity is wrong. "Doing nothing," Riccardo says in act 3, "is as bad as taking part"; and Hochhuth intends this statement to stand as a criticism of all those who stood by indifferently while the Holocaust took place.

In concentrating on Father Fontana's religious dilemma, and to a lesser extent on the career of SS Officer Kurt Gerstein, who struggled to save Jews from inside the Nazi bureaucracy, Hochhuth is deliberately directing his moral passion as a rebuke to German audiences whose participation in and indifference to the Holocaust provoked the writing of the play. One of the strengths of *The Deputy* is that Hochhuth will not permit his audiences to forget that the destruction of the six million Jews is a German problem, and so his protagonists are Christians (one German, one Italian) whose work on behalf of the Jews is portrayed as a righteous and necessary obligation despite the personal risk it involves. The Jewish characters, in particular Jacobson and the Jewish Manufacturer, also are faced with moral decisions, but such characters are relegated to a secondary status in the play and possess little psychological depth and no social influence. They become, in fact, *representative* of all oppressed people in danger, objects of concern and pity, but peripheral to the theme and action that remain faithful to Hochhuth's perspective on German (not Jewish) history and its contemporary implication. He has said:

> To look at "the mass" from outside instead of seeing oneself as part of it, an individual in the mass along with all the other individuals: it is this point of view which gives rise to the level of morality that provides the modern killers and their thoughtless pimps on every social stratum with their "intellectual" weaponry. . . . A drama that respects man as an individual does not need any further "commitment" beyond that. It's already accomplishing more than the current fashion wishes to allow.[10]

Often cited as an example of the postwar documentary style of German playwriting,[11] *The Deputy* is actually, for much of its inordinate length, a rather traditional kind of play whose dramatic ancestors, as Martin Esslin, C. D. Innes, and others have pointed out, are Schiller and Shaw.[12] The play as a whole is something of a stylistic jumble, but its problems are at least partially concealed by Hochhuth's moral outrage, intellectual discipline, and the skillful staging of several confrontations between passionate antagonists. When the moment finally arrives for Riccardo's confrontation with the Pope in act 4, we are prepared for everything except the shock of the two notorious images that summarize their personal arguments, professional situations, and historical positions: Riccardo pinning the yellow Jewish star on his black cassock, and Pius XII's washing his hands after spilling the proclamation ink on them. In these two powerful images can be seen the positive and negative history of Jews and Christians. From across generations and centuries we respond to both gestures for their revelation about character and for their historical resonance: a righteous gentile meets an heir of Pilate, and the ethical conflict of Christians during the Holocaust is revealed, but *without Jews being theatrically present.* The murder of Father Fontana at the end of *The Deputy,* a Jew by disposition and desire, underscores the increasingly obvious diminution of the Jewish presence or of positive Jewish images in the plays of Holocaust experience as dramatized by German-language playwrights. (As an individual playwright, of course, Hochhuth cannot be blamed for this situation.)

There is, however, one problem with *The Deputy* that, while understandable from the point of view of production, presents a serious confusion in the articulation of Hochhuth's ideas. The difficulty arises in the playwright's note on the casting:

> The Characters grouped together here by twos, threes, or fours, should be played by the same actor—for recent history has taught us that in the age of universal military conscription it is not necessarily to anyone's credit or blame, or even a question of character, which uniform one wears or whether one stands on the side of the victim or the executioners.

(p. 12)

Hochhuth surely means this statement to underscore his loathing of contemporary society for its conformity and ethical passivity, but the staging device he outlines also contains ambiguity and risk. This kind of double and triple casting, especially in realistically conceived scenes, presents powerful stage images that reveal how the same individual can be seen as victim and victimizer. (The subject is dealt with in chapter 4.) This is the effect, for example, of the same actor playing both Eichmann and the Jewish Manufacturer. As a result of this technique, Jewish images are transformed and confused still further. For Hochhuth, the interchangeability of the Nazis and those they murdered is never his real intention; in fact, he is sympathetic to Jews and angry at their fate. But his remarks concerning the preservation of the individual, noted above, are seriously undercut by the symbolic burdens of his characters and their apparent "interchangeability" as well.[13] *The Deputy* would seem to extend further the diminishment of the individual, and especially of the individual Jew, which is the progression I am attempting to trace.

Seventeen productions of Peter Weiss's *The Investigation* were produced concurrently throughout Europe in the fall of 1965. Like Hochhuth's play, it was subjected to outraged condemnation. Unlike Hochhuth's, it engages the Holocaust theme through a documentary form. The text of the play was taken from the transcripts of the trial of Auschwitz personnel in Frankfurt between 1963 and 1965, which Weiss then shaped according to his own political bias and theatrical preferences. In truth, the play can be (and has been) justifiably criticized for its shifting our attention away from the ethical issues that the Holocaust raises, and away from the Holocaust's victims as well. In the testimony of the 5th Witness, summarizing her camp experience, we see Weiss's strategy:

> Even as I jumped out of the freight car
> into that confusion on the platform
> I knew that what mattered here was
> to look out for yourself
> to try to work your way up
> to make a good impression
> and to keep away from anything
> that might drag you down
> When they made us lie down on the tables
> in the reception room
> and inspected our rectums
> and our sexual organs
> for concealed valuables
> every last remnant

of our usual life
vanished
Family
home
occupation
and possessions
were ideas
that were wiped out
when the number
was stamped into your arm
And already we had started to live
with a new set of values
and to adjust to this world
which for anyone
who wanted to survive in it
became a normal world
the supreme commandment was
to stay healthy
and to show you were physically strong
I stuck close to those
who were too weak
to eat their rations
so I could take their food
at the first opportunity
I didn't take my eyes off
those who were dying
if they had a better sleeping place than I
. . . .
It was normal
that everything had been stolen from us
It was normal that we stole too
. . . .
It was normal
that all around us people were dying
and it was normal
to live in the face of one's own death
Our feelings grew numb
and we looked at corpses
with complete indifference
and that was normal
And it was normal

that there were some among us
who helped those who stood over us
to beat us
. . . .
Only the cunning survived
only those who every day
with unrelenting alertness
took and held their bit of ground.[14]

The effect on audiences of this speech and others like it is problematic
and misleading. For Alvin H. Rosenfeld, the play's severest critic, *The
Investigation* is a perfect example of "the exploitation of atrocity,"
where the pain of the victim is, in performance, purposely neutralized
in order to advance the playwright's political agenda. "To [Weiss] the
ashes are so much data, the residue of a burnt-out system."[15]

   Although other critics have not been as harsh in their evaluation of
The Investigation,[16] it is hard to avoid the conclusion that Weiss has
suffered a severe failure of compassion in "putting together" his play,
an ethical flaw in this "objective" text. Weiss's deemphasis of the Jewish
experience of suffering to the point where the word *Jew* never appears
in the play, is a cruel and purposeful omission, one part of Weiss's attempt to "flatten" the human image in the play.

> . . . the point is not to depict individual conflicts, but patterns of
> socio-economic behavior. Documentary theater is only concerned
> with what is exemplary, in contrast to the quickly exhausted ex-
> ternal constellation; it does not work with stage characters and
> depictions of milieux, but with groups, force-fields, trends.[17]

The condition of identicalness between victim and oppressor becomes
pervasive as the text diminishes the emotional content of the Witnesses'
stories and denies individuality to the Jewish characters. In his "note"
to the play, Weiss warns that "no attempt should be made to re-
construct the courtroom . . . [for it would be] as impossible as trying to
present the camp itself on the stage." It is not at all clear, however,
whether these two issues should be equated, and we suspect that Weiss
may have linked them together as a way to lend support to his own
political beliefs. Our concern is heightened when Weiss specifies: "Personal experience and confrontations must be steeped in anonymity. In-
asmuch as the witnesses in the play lose their names, they become mere
speaking tubes" (p. 1). Using these instructions as a guide to production of the play causes the reality of the Jewish experience to lose its
human dimension. As full, individualized images give way to an un-

differentiated group portrait, the Holocaust becomes a mechanism for exploiting the suffering of its victims.

There is a painful irony here. Commentators on Holocaust literature have often remarked that the decimation of Europe's Jewish population during the Second World War was at least partly due to the world's inability to *feel* for the Jews' dire condition. Of course, widespread emotional indifference did not *cause* the destruction of Europe's Jewish population, but it did allow the destruction to continue up to the time of Germany's desperate surrender. *The Investigation,* in retelling the Holocaust experience, is another example of this failure of the German imagination; nowhere does it reject indifference as a permissible response to suffering and oppression, and its documentary form may even encourage it. By awarding names to the Accused but allowing the Witnesses only numbers, Weiss significantly weakens the possibility of feeling the victims' pain. In addition, he specifies that the testimony of their various, condensed experiences can be only "indicated by a change of voice or bearing," and that the actors should not "act" the characters they portray but should instead resist the temptation to create a character in a realistic sense. Thus, the Witnesses' appearance in the play, taken as a whole, creates an image of their condition in Auschwitz: anonymous victims without distinction even in their individual suffering. Weiss's indictment of the capitalist system of the West for having produced Auschwitz, besides being dubious in the extreme, has produced a stage play of remarkably callous proportions, perhaps an ironic monument to the Marxist system he prefers.

A comparison of Hochhuth's detailed, emotionally overwrought condemnation of German (and traditionally Christian) society, and Weiss's austere, emotionally constricted portrayal of institutionalized economic structures as seen through dehumanized creatures, reveals the variety and complexity of playwrights' responses to the Holocaust. Both plays minimize their attention to Jewish suffering. Weiss's play, unlike Hochhuth's, however, reflects a refusal to extend to the slaughtered millions the compassion and concern befitting their brutal mass destruction. The loss of this generosity represents a constriction of imagination and sympathy, and their replacement by a political ideology does too little to guard against the problems inherent in abstracting and universalizing human suffering—a problem that may be at the root of the German relationship to the Jewish Holocaust.[18]

Rainer Fassbinder's *Garbage, the City and Death* was written in the mid-1970s, a decade after Weiss's play, and has a rather notorious history in Germany. Most recently, in 1985, members of Frankfurt's

Jewish community, angered by plans to give the play its belated premiere, prevented its performance by sitting down on the stage at the Kammerspiel; to date, the play has yet to receive a professional production in Germany.[19]

Although it is not strictly a play dealing with the Holocaust experience, the recent controversy over Fassbinder's play proved its ability to raise many of the same issues that Holocaust dramas engage, not the least of which has been the question I am pursuing: how Jews are (and should be) pictured on the stage in the Federal Republic. Certainly Fassbinder, a thirty-year-old "bad boy" of the German art world at the time he wrote what was to be his last play (he died in 1982), was fully aware of the volatility of its subject matter, although there are reports that even he, so used to outraging the sensibilities of German audiences, was surprised by the shocked response he received from across the political spectrum.[20]

Despite its supposed basis in an actual real-estate scandal in Frankfurt in the 1970s, *Garbage, the City and Death* is a surreal play. In character and setting, it is filled with brutish and violent images expressed in the most graphic language and action. It is a play of unrelieved bleakness, populated by prostitutes, pimps, criminals, ex-Nazis, the physically deformed and infirm, and the Rich Jew, who is also an extortionist and a murderer. (Fassbinder was said to have modeled this character after a wealthy Frankfurt Jew who made a fortune in land speculation in one of the city's urban renewal projects.)

Defenders of the play generally rested their case on two arguments, one textual, one legal and cultural. The latter defense, claiming that a free society needs to have a theatre without censorship, was no more effective in gaining a hearing for the play than was the former, which argues that the character of the Rich Jew is, in fact, one of only two sympathetic characters in the play and, in context, represents the immoral—but only possible—response to an economic and political system (capitalism) based on greed, corruption, and cruelty.

How representative the Rich Jew is of *all* Jews is a question with several answers. In his own behalf, the character describes himself thus:

> . . . I'm a Jew. The police chief is my friend, in the broad sense of a friend; the mayor invites me over. I can count on the city council. No one particularly likes what he condones, but it's not my plan, it was there before I came. I have to be indifferent if children cry, if

the old and the feeble suffer. I must be indifferent. And when some people scream in a rage I quite simply ignore it. What should I do otherwise? Burden my hunched back with a bad conscience? Develop sores? Suffer the plague? I believe in God, but in justice between four walls? Should my soul stand erect for the decisions of others that I only carry out with profit which I need in order to get what I need? . . . The city needs the unscrupulous businessman who allows it to transform itself.[21]

To see this character—who enriches himself by trading on the Holocaust guilt of non-Jews, conspires with the corrupt city administration to conceal his multiple crimes, strangles the young prostitute with his necktie, and is said to possess prodigious and perverse sexual power—as a sympathetic figure is no small achievement, and it is unclear if Fassbinder intended to have the Rich Jew portrayed in a way that would brighten the loathsome and unredeemed picture of a loveless wasteland of a world. As Gerald Rabkin points out, "the play as a political critique is totally overwhelmed by a vision of thanatopia."[22]

Combining the phantasmagorical and fearsome vision of Büchner with the theatrical style of Brecht at his most despairing, the play as a whole presents an image of human degradation amid total social breakdown. True to his world view, Fassbinder's anti-Semitic images are entirely consistent with his equally odious pictures of women, gays, handicapped people, and other minorities. He is not concerned with character, plot, or setting in any traditional sense, but with the creation of images, many of which are curiously derived from the theatre itself (notably opera and dance), and which, in the context they are placed in, are defiled like everything else. The images are empowered by Fassbinder's own narcissistic self-loathing and dynamic theatricality. They are able, if recent controversy is any proof, to arouse rage to the point of hysteria—and this is no small achievement either, albeit a dubious one under the circumstances. *Garbage, the City and Death* is a shameless and cruel play exploiting its audiences' fears and anxieties in a similar way that the inhabitants of the play's moonworld exploit each other. It may be a perversely courageous play in its determination to adhere to so horrible a vision of the world, but it is not a good or honest play, because in losing the coherence of and control over its own images it becomes the evidence of the thing it seeks to excoriate: the easy, nasty, savage way people do harm to each other.

The answer to James Leverett's inquiry about Fassbinder's play: "is it anti-Semitic or does it flush out anti-Semitism?" is probably: yes to both.[23] The drama, even in its most nonrepresentational form, is symbolic of people and places. Gerald Rabkin explains:

> To lable [*sic*] it an anti-Semitic play is not the same as to say that it is a deliberate provocation in its utilizing of traditional anti-Semitic elements. We have to recognize that Fassbinder consciously utilizes elements of the anti-Semitic tradition because figures on a stage are exemplary.[24]

In *Garbage, the City and Death,* in a kind of a rewrite of Shylock's "Hath not a Jew . . . ?" speech, even the Rich Jew admits that he too is sometimes afraid. The speech is intended, one supposes, to reach audiences in their deepest selves, after exposing the garbage and death that fill the cities they inhabit. But to Jews who, after surviving the Holocaust, are diminished in nearly everything except their will to survive, images such as these will be rejected as intolerable for their anti-Semitism and for the suggestion that Fassbinder's moonlike planet is the one they live on now, rather than the one they escaped *from* a generation ago.

Primarily known as a novelist in America, the Austrian Thomas Bernhard is also a playwright of considerable renown and seems to occupy an unusual place among his colleagues. C. D. Innes, in his comprehensive review of modern German playwriting, concludes that only Bernhard can be unhesitatingly seen as lacking a political commitment in his writing.[25] From his perspective as a detached if mordant observer, Bernhard seems to have attracted German-speaking audiences with ironic pictures of their country in the grip of inertia and terminal decline. Admirers of his work appreciate especially the kind of mockery of German culture that they find in his plays. *Eve of Retirement* is reported to be Bernhard's most popular play and has been described as "a comedy of the German soul."[26] One approving critic sums up his bizarre attributes:

> Bernhard is a master of insult and a diatriber of apparently inexhaustible tenacity. He already has readers, addicts almost, who get strength and comfort from uplifting sermons.[27]

Eve of Retirement is a three-character drama set in the home of Rudolf Hoeller, a chief justice and former concentration camp head, on an evening before his retirement when, alone with his two sisters, he celebrates Heinrich Himmler's birthday. The theatrical enactment of this annual event is a savage comment on the Nazi sympathies of respectable German bourgeoisie, past and present, who, as represented in the play, furtively engage in the full range of human depravity, from racism to incest. The Hoellers' condition is one of sour impotence enlivened by the paranoid whine of their complaint against anyone unlike them. An evening in their company would seem to provide audiences with a singularly depressing experience, despite the comedy that might be discovered in what one critic called the play's "absurd realism." "This script is superior," he writes,

> at least for an intellectual audience, to every other antifascist play, written with the best of intentions, precisely because it derives its acute impact from the unintentional, unscrupulous self-evident manner in which the sarcastic, nihilistic Thomas Bernhard treats his characters, whether victims or perpetrators.[28]

No Holocaust play, however, has the luxury of being written unintentionally, and treating the Holocaust's victims identically with the Holocaust perpetrators is an aesthetic choice with serious ethical implications, liable to historical and critical repudiation. Despite the fact that no Jews appear in Bernhard's crepuscular world of moral blindness and social decay, their presence is often referred to and, in fact, is demanded by the nature of the play's action. It is hard to imagine the kind of laughter this "comedy" would provoke other than a meanspirited, condescending chuckle. Nevertheless, it is unlikely that *Eve* is intended as a parody of realism, and it would take a lighter and more wholesome comic gift than Bernhard seems to possess to view the play from that perspective. Hoeller is an unrepentant anti-Semite whose opinions are given no rebuttal.

> The good German detests what is going on
> in this country
> Depravity hypocrisy general stupefaction
> The Jewish element has taken root everywhere.
> (p. 112)

(Nor is refutation to be found in the mild irony of Rudolf's sister Vera's telephoning the despised Jewish doctor to attend to Rudolf after his heart attack at the play's conclusion.)

An appropriate response to *Eve of Retirement* would surely include perturbation as to why so smug and nasty a play should have achieved such popularity, as well as to question the usefulness of negative images when dealing with the destruction of European Jewry.[29] In act 3, while Beethoven is played at dinner, Vera remarks:

> Oh Rudolf will we live to see the day
> I don't think it will take too long
> until we can openly confess to what we are
> until justice returns
> to the world once again.
>
> (p. 184)

Bernhard's world, a humorless mix of Strindberg and Beckett, is as repulsive as Fassbinder's, though more upscale. It lacks the sense of compassion that makes Strindberg and Beckett valuable to us, not to say morally relevant. Without Jews on the stage of *Eve of Retirement,* and with the derogatory statements made about them in their absence, we have another example of modern German drama's difficulty in confronting the past, specifically the Jewish question, without images of insult and strategies of evasion. Taken together, these aesthetic characteristics show an ethical lapse not completely hidden by the flatness of Bernhard's satire. "It is his impending retirement I fear," says Vera, "then all of us will be sitting here in this room just waiting to die" (p. 151). But it is unclear if Hoeller's retirement will signal their quick demise along with the evil they represent, or merely that their eminently comfortable middle-class lives, indicators of their generation's social and economic success, will be lost without the protection of Rudolf's professional status as a dispenser of a neo-Nazi ideology and justice. Lacking a clear point of view on questions of ethics, *Eve of Retirement* seems to conclude that the German legacy of the Holocaust is one of unfinished business and personal inconvenience.

Heinar Kipphardt's *Brother Eichmann* (1983), like his earlier play, *In the Matter of J. Robert Oppenheimer* (1964), is an important example of the documentary theatre form, and it portrays the Holocaust experience, which he first dealt with in *Joel Brand* (1965). The story of *Joel Brand* concerned the aborted "deal" Adolf Eichmann proposed late in the war to trade Hungarian Jews for trucks. Kipphardt's return to the Eichmann character in the 1980s was surely motivated by the contemporary events he notes in the course of the play. While ostensibly focusing on Eichmann's detention and execution in the early 1960s, Kipphardt is able to provide an extraordinarily wide panorama of recent

German and world history with the objective of producing an indictment of Western moral values. In this he is exceedingly skillful, a master of the documentary form of theatre whose "real aim," notes C. D. Innes, is "to produce political action, if only in the form of discussion, rather than aesthetic appreciation. . . ."[30]

The two acts of *Brother Eichmann*[31] are set in the Israeli prison where Eichmann was incarcerated after his kidnapping in Argentina. The first part precedes his trial, and the second takes place after the trial and concludes with his execution. The prison scenes of both parts are interspersed with other factual and imagined episodes located in various countries between 1933 and 1983. These "analogy scenes" provide the play with its scope, its relevance, and its controversy. For example, between scenes 2 and 3 of part 1, we hear on tape "a very serious, very plausible sequence from a Hitler speech dealing with the world economic crisis." The seventh scene is comprised of five "analogies": (1) painful testimony of a Japanese atomic bomb victim who describes his agony in front of a film of an atomic explosion; (2) an "American expert" declaring his preference for clean neutron bombs over dirty nuclear ones; (3) two staged interviews from an American documentary movie, "The Nuclear Battlefield," showing two American officers speaking matter-of-factly about the destruction of Europe if atomic weapons are used against the Soviet Union; (4) a film interview with an American bomber pilot who flies missions over Southeast Asia, following orders and ignoring moral complications; and (5) a speech by a genetic engineer describing his work creating the perfect gene pool for future citizens. When interspersed between the Eichmann scenes, these analogous "factual" references have the intended effect of universalizing Eichmann's crimes against humanity and validating Kipphardt's anti-American and antimilitarist views. In this highly politicized context, we are urged to accept that Eichmann is, in fact, the brother of us all.

The most volatile aspect of *Brother Eichmann* lies in its comparison of Nazi atrocities against the Jews to Israel's actions against the Arab population surrounding it. In part 1, scene 9, episode "e," an Israeli soldier describes his recurring dream of himself as a Nazi soldier mistreating Arabs in the way the Germans abused his murdered Polish parents. The five episodes of scene 5, part 2 deal with General Ariel Sharon's involvement in the 1982 massacre at the Palestinean refugee camps in Lebanon, including his justification of the atrocities in response to negative Israeli and world opinion. The effect of these scenes is more striking than truthful. First, we are urged to believe that the Israelis are today's Nazis, and that the fascist tendencies that produce world terrorism are to be found dominating the governments of all western "progressive" countries, including the United States, Italy, and, of course, Germany. (Scene 17 of part 2 is a sympathetic treatment of the Red Brigades and the Baader-Meinhof Gang.)

These malicious images of the interchangeability of the Holocaust victims with the murderous victimizers is extended into the Eichmann scenes as well. In part 1, scene 13, the Israeli police captain, Less, confesses (with some anguish) that he feels himself closer to Eichmann every day. In part 2, scene 6, Eichmann's wife, Vera, calls him the true "scapegoat" and tells him how their son, hearing of his father's conviction by the Israeli court, exclaimed "How can you believe in a just God after this?"—a question often asked by the survivors of concentration camps. In addition, there is the irresponsible congruence of Arab victims of Jewish terror to Jewish victims of Nazi terror.

The second effect of *Brother Eichmann* is to revise the image of Eichmann along the lines of Hannah Arendt's understanding of him in her *Eichmann in Jerusalem.* But Kipphardt goes further and is more successful than Arendt, not only because the live stage image of Eichmann is so much more immediate and powerful than the prose version of him, but because Kipphardt intends to invent and stress qualities in Eichmann's character that are sympathetic, positive, and even "Jewish" in his persecution. In fact, over the course of the play, while Eichmann is *in Israeli custody,* he changes from a precise, prudish, and morally obtuse criminal (his faults, as Kipphardt shows them), to a loving, responsible, and principled victim of the Jewish need to revenge the crimes of the Holocaust. Nowhere is this more explicit than in the final, almost comic image of part 1, when the informally dressed Eichmann (in baggy pants and checkered slippers), helpless and isolated, is highlighted in a sudden (and unmotivated) volley of flashbulbs. This occurs immediately after we have watched an eight-minute film of Nazi atrocities *along with him* and *through him* because he has been positioned *facing the screen* between the audience and the film image. "Look at this confused, unfortunate, silly fellow," we are urged to think, "hounded by the forces of revenge and hypocrisy, but really quite harmless." He is, in Kipphardt's bizarre reversal, a kind of Nazi Adam Kurtzik.

The final six scenes of *Brother Eichmann* show the prisoner preparing for his execution, and they are pacific, nearly sentimental scenes. The action is moved along by the recurrent visits of Pastor and Mrs.

Hull, two Canadian Protestants determined to bring the condemned man to a religious salvation he protests he has long since found. Declaring himself unrepentant and at peace, Eichmann is hanged in the prison that, for Kipphardt, stands for all Israel, wearing a bright red suit, after which his body falls into the earth and disappears. So much for where and how this now harmless "devil" comes to rest, according to the images presented to us. The extended final speech, delivered by the good if ineffectual Reverend Hull, describes in meticulous detail how he identified Eichmann's body, watched it being cremated (which reminds him of how the Jews were burned in the Holocaust), and then supervised the ashes being thrown into the sea "to await the day of resurrection" (p. 160). The ambiguity of this future event is left unremarked on by Kipphardt, but, in the light of history, even revisionist history, it gives cause for concern. It is a distinctly different resurrection from the one Sylvanus, with biblical assistance, envisioned in *Dr. Korczak and the Children.*

II

In this survey of six postwar German-language plays, it is possible to discern a theatrical paradigm with historical, aesthetic, and political implications. As the Nazi attempt to destroy Europe's Jewish population becomes dimmer in memory, the complexity of its relationship to contemporary Germans seems to exert an even stronger confrontational pressure. In Anson Rabinbach's words: "If it is no longer possible to speak of a German-Jewish symbiosis, it is, ironically, still possible to speak of a 'Jewish question' in Germany today."[32] Germany's Jewish population, numbering about twenty-five thousand today, has significance and influence totally incommensurate to its size, for which the events of the Holocaust are largely responsible. The situation of Jews in Germany in the 1980s, though perhaps less precarious than in other countries from an economic and political standpoint, is nonetheless characterized by psychological anxiety and social uneasiness. Forty-three years after the war, both Germans and Jews still are trying to find ways to come to terms with their mutual past and their problematic future. German-language playwrights attempt to define this relationship.

For the last two generations of Germans who grew up after the war, the question of guilt and responsibility over the "final solution" naturally assumes a more abstract place, and, in an altered context from that of their parents or grandparents, the Holocaust becomes a metaphor for other realities closer in time and urgency. As C. D. Innes has written in his introduction to *Modern German Drama:*

> We find that these concentration camps or revolutionary situations are not the subjects of the plays but symbols, examples through which general questions can be analyzed. . . .
>   . . . the issues that arise . . . are translated into global terms . . . to the extent that the details are too alien for the immediate audience to understand and the meaning becomes so generalized that special techniques are required if German spectators are to apply the points to their own context.[33]

Whether these techniques are called "documentary theatre" or "absurd realism" or "nihilistic theatricalism" (my term), they all represent dramaturgical attempts to confront audiences with present realities through a juxtaposition with Germany's Nazi past.

But there is a great social and psychological disservice that can be done to the victims of the Holocaust by a playwright's uncertain understanding, callous disregard, or political attachments. In this lamentable situation, Weiss's *The Investigation* can be seen as a pivotal contribution to the process of deflecting concern away from the history of Jews through a process of aesthetic dehumanization. The shocking and ironic result of Weiss's artistic (and of course, political) decisions, ones shared by Fassbinder, Bernhard, and Kipphardt, though manifested in different ways, is to revitalize irresponsible and dangerous images of Jews, the like of which may have contributed to German participation or acquiescence in the Jews' destruction. Even when these images (once so positive in Sylvanus and even Hochhuth) are somewhat less than central to the playwright's political agenda, they arrive at the same stereotypical and dangerous place, as in *Brother Eichmann.* This is the inevitable result of making a metaphor of the Holocaust: it diminishes the nature (and understanding) of the crimes committed and the responsibility of those who committed the crimes, as well as the humanity of those who suffered most because of those crimes.

German drama, like the German-speaking nations, has a unique relationship to the Holocaust; all kinds of people have all kinds of reasons either to keep it in public view or to bury it forever. The historical record of Nazi behavior toward Jews (and other persecuted peoples) creates a volatile theatrical context for plays that deal with those events. For this reason, the plays will have an effect on German audiences markedly different from their effect on non-German ones. But we must be careful to distinguish between legitimate artistic ambiguities and unacceptable evasions when dealing with the moral issues raised by the Holocaust. Although the complete truth about the Holocaust can never be grasped, we should always be alert to the kind of exploitation that appears whenever easy irony or superficial analogy usurps the concern for humanity or a humane destiny. There is, I believe, an unintended irony in Kipphardt's use of Pascal's statement as his epigraph for *Brother Eichmann:* "Never does one do wrong so thoroughly and well as when one does so with a clear conscience."

There is another remarkable similarity in *The Investigation* and the three plays that follow it in my discussion. All four reveal a combination of despair and self-hatred. The cheapness of life in modern times, a condition seemingly validated by the Holocaust, is a historical and contemporary premise these plays begin from and articulate. None advances a program or image to oppose this situation. Perhaps, in a terrible way, the Holocaust has done its evil work by defeating the humane impulses in many people. German-language dramatists may even be contributing to the conditions they deplore by writing plays where "the individual is missing," an understandable condition when "practically the only approach not evident in serious German drama of the last twenty years is the conventional naturalistic form."[34]

I would never advocate a return to the bankruptcy of strict realism, but I cannot help but feel that one feature of the realistic form might provide us with a lesson about Holocaust drama that we could find useful. Realism's preoccupation with characters who are psychologically complex and recognizably human might provide an extended range of Holocaust drama, and especially of the images of Jews whose abstracted "invisible presence" in most of German drama and German society is the condition that provoked this discussion.

Six

Responses and Responsibilities

Words and eggs must be handled with
care.
Once broken they are impossible
things to repair.

           —Anne Sexton, "Words"

THERE is no basis any longer for speaking of the Holocaust as un-imaginable for, in addition to the historical fact that it was imagined by the German state fifty years ago, it has been reimagined in artistic fact innumerable times since. What standards should be used to determine the achievement of a piece of Holocaust literature and, in particular, a Holocaust drama? Aside from the general observation that no serious artistic work of any kind can succeed if it lacks technical skill, human insight, and moral passion, in the case of drama there is an additional requirement of a sensitive and disciplined production. In this final chapter, I want to expand upon the two additional criteria regarding theatrical approaches to the Holocaust that I discussed in previous chapters, for they deeply influence how we respond to and evaluate Holocaust drama. First, no Holocaust drama can be successful if it demeans the suffering or memory of the mass of Holocaust victims; and, second, no Holocaust drama can be successful if it distorts or denies history for the purpose of advancing otherwise unrelated causes.[1]

There is a need, of course, to specify what is meant by successful. (I do not mean commercial success, although a few plays and a number of films have succeeded in this way.) An excellent definition is suggested by Peter Demetz:

In the long run, our discussion of what kind of writing should be appropriate to the age of Auschwitz is totally irrelevant, if it touches on issues of genre alone and does not look for the presence of compassion. I cannot believe that categories of tradition and experimentation, realism and surrealism are more important than the individual text, in whatever mode, as long as it prevents us from believing that Auschwitz was just another event in world history.[2]

The meaningful connection between practical and ethical criteria is a helpful guide to finding standards by which to evaluate Holocaust drama. It is this kind of a connection I have argued for and stressed in this book. One benefit of keeping it in mind is that it becomes easier to distinguish between bad productions of good Holocaust dramas and good productions of bad plays that engage the Holocaust experience.

I

In the previous chapters, I have discussed a number of plays that either adhere to or neglect the critical standards I have suggested. In chapter 4, I discussed the irresponsible motives of several plays that present pernicious images of interchangeable personalities between the Nazis and their victims. In chapter 5, I noted how selected German writers of the 1970s and 1980s (Fassbinder, Bernhardt, Kipphardt) have chosen to diminish the presence and the importance of Jews and Jewish experience, preferring instead to show images that degrade Jews (and others), exculpate Germans, or excoriate everyone. A majority of the other playwrights I have discussed have rejected the sensational and exploitative depictions of the Holocaust and have written plays that are moving and profound meditations on crucial human issues. The appropriateness of the work of the Liebermans (*Throne of Straw*), Sobol (*Ghetto*), Delbo (*Who Will Carry the Word?*), and others discussed in the early chapters of this book, are examples of the best in Holocaust drama and of any drama: they are generous and rigorous in their retelling of the Holocaust story, and although they may pass harsh judgments or possess grave reservations about human action, their respect for history and desire for understanding is never in doubt. One play I have not considered thus far offers a difficult test for my criteria concerning the evaluation of this ever-growing body of work I have called elsewhere the theatre of the Holocaust. It is a drama of considerable skill and compassion, but with significant flaws as well, and I discuss it now because its ambiguous achievement poses the clearest example of the problems encountered in the criticism of Holocaust drama.

Martin Sherman's *Bent*,[3] produced first in England in May 1979, and in America later that year, has as its theme the treatment of homosexuals in Nazi Germany. The six scenes of the first act move us from the apartment of two homosexuals, Rudy and Max, to the backstage dressing room of a sleazy nightclub, to a park, a forest, a train, and finally to the barracks of a concentration camp where Max is taken after his arrest as a criminal deviant under the laws of the Third Reich. Into these scenes the playwright skillfully compresses the story of gay oppression in Germany and establishes the sense of real danger and terror that homosexuals endured at the hands of the Nazis. (Sherman appends to the text of the play a brief chronology of the conditions of homosexuals in Germany from 1871 to 1936.)[4]

The first act of *Bent* starts Max on a painful journey to self-understanding for which the Holocaust provides the social and political context. Max is violently uprooted from the security of social indifference to his sexual orientation in pre–Hitler Germany, and he is deposited in the dangerous and degrading venue provided by the Nazis for all those who didn't, or couldn't, conform to the rules of "Aryan purity." The problem with *Bent* first appears in the scene in the barracks, when Max explains to his fellow prisoner Horst how he was able to attain a more privileged status than was possible for a "pink triangle" in the concentration camp. (Homosexuals were identified by that badge sewn on their jackets.)

> HORST: . . . . How'd you get the yellow star?
> MAX: I'm Jewish.
> HORST: You're not Jewish, you're a queer. [*Silence.*]
> MAX: I didn't want one.
> HORST: Didn't want one?
> MAX: A pink triangle.
> HORST: Didn't *want* one?
> MAX: You told me it was the lowest. So I didn't want one.
> HORST: So?
> MAX: I worked a deal.
> HORST: A deal?
> MAX: Sure. I'm good at that.
> HORST: With the Gestapo?
> MAX: Sure.

HORST: You're full of shit.
MAX: [. . .] And they said . . . prove that you're . . . and I did . . .
HORST: Prove that you're what?
MAX: Not.
HORST: Not what?
MAX: Queer.
HORST: How?
MAX: Her.
HORST: Her?
MAX: They said, if you . . . and I did . . .
HORST: Did what?
MAX: Her. Made . . .
HORST: Made what?
MAX: Love.
HORST: Who to?
MAX: Her.
HORST: Who was she?
MAX: Only . . . maybe . . . maybe only thirteen . . . she was
maybe . . . she was dead. . . .

MAX: I proved that I wasn't . . . [*Silence.*] And they enjoyed it.
HORST: Yes.
MAX: And I said, I'm not queer. And they laughed. And I said,
give me a yellow star. And they said, sure, make him a Jew. He's
not bent. And they laughed. They were having fun. But . . . I . . .
got . . . my . . . star.
HORST: [*Gently.*] Oh yes.
MAX: I got my star.

Max's victory, of course, because it comes at the price of denying his
homosexuality, is, according to Sherman, meant to be understood by
us and, eventually by Max, as nothing less than self-annihilation.
   The playwright carefully structures the first act of *Bent* to conclude
with Max's extraordinary and horrifying revelation of how he "got his
star." He intends the shock to sustain our interest over the intermission, and to firmly establish the primacy of his deeply felt argument:
that if gays conceal their sexual nature, they destroy their identity and
do their oppressors' work. Max's yellow star keeps him safe (according
to Sherman), but at the same time condemns him to a life more degraded than Jews or gays endure because his safety and privilege are
based on a personal lie. (That homosexuals were treated worse than

Jews may also be a lie, but it is the assumption upon which Sherman's play is based.) At the end of *Bent,* Sherman is explicit in his advocacy of gay identity at any cost; he intends Max's real victory to come at last with his suicide on the electrified wire surrounding the camp compound.

The real problem with Max's situation concerns the premise that sees his survival in terms of its relationship to another set of Holocaust victims, the Jews. *Bent* seems to lapse from its passionate call for justice and freedom for gays, and to decline into a melodramatic love story based on a needless argument about which outlawed group suffered more under the Nazis. This is the impression given by Max's final gesture, one that is intended to certify and celebrate Max's new confidence in and appreciation of himself through the rejection of the "easy" Jewish existence.

> MAX *climbs out of the pit* [*where* HORST's *body was thrown*].
> MAX *holds* HORST's *jacket with the pink triangle on it. Puts the jacket on.*
> MAX *turns and looks at the fence.*
> MAX *walks into the fence.*
> *The fence lights up. It grows brighter and brighter, until the light consumes the stage.*
> *And blinds the audience.*

To be sure, the "blinding" of the audience as a result of an on-stage electrocution is a highly theatrical method of killing. It also is intended to make the audience "see" what they have been ignorant of: the history of gays before and during the Holocaust and, as a result, the oppression of gays today in a society that is more free and tolerant. In addition, and I think of greater importance to Sherman, the sudden bright light validates the "brilliance" of Max's love for Horst and underscores the shock of the recognition Max achieves concerning his true nature. But unlike the situation in *The Cannibals* or *Who Will Carry the Word?,* we do not see Max's suicide as inevitable or even necessary. In those two plays, choosing death over cannibalism or murder is made to seem both horrifying and inescapable, but those qualities are less available to a suicide committed for want of a lost love and a need to publicly proclaim a forbidden sexual preference. Max's action places him closer to Krause in *Resort 76,* dying for shame and disappointment, than it does to Uncle or Haas (whose father was a homosexual) in Tabori's play, or Gina in Delbo's. The world does not seem well lost for Max, and in taking his own life, he actually seems weaker than Horst, who dies while attempting to assault the Nazi captain.

Bent concludes with an image that ambiguously illuminates several attitudes of its playwright. In order to present the case for gay liberation and provide positive stage images of homosexual behavior, Sherman has imagined a situation that instead diminishes the urgency and correctness of his cause. He distorts the Holocaust experience and deflects our attention away from the terrible suffering of all the Nazis' victims whose humanity was destroyed. This is not to say that the Holocaust "belongs to the Jews," a mistaken argument I totally reject, but that Sherman's considerable skill, insight, and passion does not do justice—cannot do justice—to the reductive nature of his drama. Ultimately, *Bent* is not successful because it is not truthful to the larger cause that would validate his smaller one.

A capable production of *Bent,* despite its problematical text, is not impossible to imagine, one which deemphasizes the sensational staging the play seems to call for and finds its power in the restrained but full commitment of able actors sensitive to the needs of characters in danger and distress. The New York production, however, was a disaster: a star performer doing turns for a coterie audience and most of the other actors standing outside their characters and above their material. The most memorable moment at the performance I attended was not the final, sudden "blinding through illumination" (and vice versa), or the sensational scene in the second act when Max and Horst, standing ten feet apart and facing the audience, achieve mutual orgasm through exclusively verbal stimuli. The moment of special interest involved one of the physical aspects of the second-act design:

> *A large fence extends across the stage. In front of the fence, on one side, lies a pile of rocks. On the other side—far over—a deep pit.*

> MAX *is moving rocks. He carries one rock from the pile to the other side and starts a new pile. He returns and takes another rock. The rocks are carried one by one. He wears a prison uniform and hat.*

In fact, the New York actor playing Max, in addition to uniform and hat, was wearing *a pair of gloves* to protect his hands from the stones, and in that single detail (among numerous others) was contained the destruction of the theatrical premise and historical basis of the realistic Holocaust setting: the unrelenting and total barbarity of the Nazis. In such ways can small lies at the edge of a production confuse or damage the larger meanings at its center.

Plays of the Holocaust experience must painstakingly build a sense of trust between playwright and audience, and that trust, if threatened or contradicted by inappropriate textual or production decisions, cannot be easily restored. For one audience member, *Bent* violated that trust, and less than successfully met its artistic and moral obligations. Of course, the nature of trust between playwright and audience is reciprocal. As audience members, we must be prepared to bestow that trust as our part in the theatrical relationship of playgoing when it is honestly requested through a truthful performance. Whereas it is easy for a playwright (or director) to break that trust, it is equally hard for some audiences to grant trust because they have expectations and prejudices about the Holocaust material before they encounter it on stage. The problem of not being prepared to receive the dramatic material or to fairly acknowledge the author's perspective, afflicts all people to some degree and is an especially prevalent condition in the reception of Holocaust drama. An audience must greet Holocaust drama with openness, generosity, and concern, despite an awareness of the frequent exploitation of the material. The pitfalls of viewing too narrowly is the last important matter I wish to discuss in this book, because it points to a universal problematic attitude that can strongly affect the reception of Holocaust drama. The condition is summed up in a remark of Lawrence Langer's: "We must embrace various and often contradictory viewpoints in our efforts to understand the event we call the Holocaust."[5]

To define this issue as clearly as possible, I want to depart from the material of Holocaust drama and concentrate on a treatment of the Holocaust experience in film. Because the problem is as much a critical one as a textual one, where the difficulty is found not in the art object but in the reception of it and response to it, the shift in forms is both useful and justifiable. In addition, the film in question is not unrelated to the material presented in chapter 1, and, I am comfortable ending my speculations at the same place where I began. Lastly, because the film is available to be seen in a permanent form (unlike a theatre piece, which is ever-changing), the ideas I express here can be tested and judged by the readers of this book.

In my discussion of the issues of survival and choice, I referred to the critical dispute between Bruno Bettelheim and Terrence Des Pres, and their disagreement over the meaning and implications of Lina

Wertmuller's film *Seven Beauties*. Although I do not support completely Des Pres's contentions about the film, I cannot agree with Bettelheim's opinions at all, and not only because I am unsympathetic to his conclusions about how life had to be lived in the concentration camps. My own objections to Bettelheim's analysis are rooted in his insistence on seeing Wertmuller's film from a restrictive and doctrinaire position that misperceives and misrepresents the nature of her achievement. Bettelheim's hostile response to *Seven Beauties* was determined by what he wanted to see, and that prevented him from receiving what the filmmaker actually did. There is much provocative material in his analysis, and also much to avoid in his critical approach to the film (and, by extension, to Holocaust drama).[6]

Seven Beauties is the ironic nickname of a handsome, petty thug named Pasqualino whose story Wertmuller tells. We follow his escapades as a womanizer, rapist, and murderer in his prewar Italian neighborhood, in a mental hospital, in a concentration camp, and finally, after the camp's liberation by the Americans, in the streets of his town again. In assessing Wertmuller's view of Pasqualino's career, Bettelheim falls into several traps that are the inevitable results of the rigidity of his artistic preferences and his historical and psychological perspectives. First, he refuses to consider any place for comedy in the artistic treatment of Holocaust issues. Second, he has no patience with ambiguity of any kind and rejects any treatment of the Holocaust whose argument is indirect or ironic. Third, as a price for critical acceptance, he insists on the presentation of images of heroism in the fight against evil, heroism that, even in defeat, represents an assertion of meaning and value in an otherwise squalid universe. In short, Bettelheim advocates the melodramatization of the Holocaust, into which Wertmuller's wholly different perspective and intent cannot be accommodated. For example, he writes:

> But in this film the senseless banality of evil is so forcibly impressed on us, and is so inextricably interwoven with the comic, that evil loses nearly all its impact. While the horrors of war, Fascism, and the concentration camp are clearly and overtly presented, covertly they are much more effectively denied, because what we watch is a farce played in a charnel house, and, furthermore, because survival despite evil and survival through doing evil seem to be in the end all-important, regardless of the form that either the evil or the survival takes. . . . But in this film we are made to feel that human dignity is a sham, because when we en-

counter its assertion in the concentration camp we are first much taken by it, but then are given to understand that it is senseless. This is not because those who act with dignity are destroyed or destroy themselves but because their destruction happens in a ridiculous way.[7]

The crippling narrowness of Bettelheim's vision is easily seen in his discussions of three incidents from the film. Early in his essay, he analyzes the effect of the movie's extraordinary beginning: the upbeat, jazzy music (with the sardonic narration repeating the refrain "Oh, yeah") counterpointing the documentary images of the ravages of modern warfare. "The song is mockingly comic rather than tragic, and so robs the scenes of war and destruction of much of their impact. And Mussolini and Hitler are so pompous that we cannot take them seriously."[8] Later in his essay, Bettelheim begins his meditation on the nature of Pasqualino's survival in the concentration camp. "It is the depiction of the survivor that robs survivorship of all meaning. It makes seeing the film an experience which degrades."[9] At the end of his essay, Bettelheim discusses the appearance of a copy of Bronzino's beautiful painting *Venus, Cupid, Folly and Time* in the room of the hideously fat camp commandant, the repulsive woman Pasqualino must sexually (if pathetically) assault if he wishes to gain the status and privilege of a kapo. Bettelheim lists four possible meanings for the appearance of the painting, and he concludes his speculations in language that is characterized by a dismissive mixture of perplexity and contempt.[10]

In all three incidents (and others besides), Bettelheim has misjudged Wertmuller. He refuses to consider any interpretation of the film that jeopardizes his understanding of the Holocaust and his preferences for its artistic treatment. If he were responsive to Wertmuller's satirical irony, and willing to consider her grotesque kind of black comedy as something other than a mockery of the Holocaust and its survivors, *Seven Beauties* would strike him as a very different film.

A different perspective on the film reveals Pasqualino as the representative of survivors who learn nothing from their camp experience because they were and are incapable of making moral distinctions. It is true that he agrees to (and even invents) any loathsome action in order to survive (including shooting his only friend), but his behavior does not necessarily diminish the survivorship of those Bettelheim encountered or heard about during the time of his own incarceration. (Of course, Bettelheim sees *himself* as a representative of the kind of positive survivorship he demands, and is personally offended by the portrayal of Pasqualino.) Pasqualino represents the guiltless, amoral, misogynistic, criminal (and gentile) survivors who existed alongside (and over) the more "positive," heroic examples of the aggressive self-sacrifice that Bettelheim prefers, indeed demands.[11] In the theatre, Pasqualino would be recognized as a descendent of characters Ibsen or Pirandello wrote about (Engstrand in *Ghosts* and Mortensgaard in *Rosmersholm* or Belcredi in *Henry IV*), characters whose unscrupulous opportunism and moral obtuseness always permit them to land on their feet. But just as it would be mistaken to conclude that *Ghosts* advocates the ideal of "honesty is the worst policy" because of its outcome, so it would be incorrect to assume that *Seven Beauties* is advocating the idea that survival at any price is correct. In fact, Wertmuller is showing us evil at work, and I believe she condemns it, but she does so obliquely, with a derisive tone and enough mischievous ambiguity to confuse and outrage critics who are unable to acknowledge an alternative perspective (and I think a justifiable and humane one) on the Holocaust.

With a broader and more flexible outlook, Bettelheim might have been able to see the opening sequence of *Seven Beauties* as a series of sounds and images that warn critics *not* to expect the traditional artistic modes of Holocaust investigation, a sequence that taunts the viewer with a seductive invitation to explore old problems in new ways. Putting jazzy music and filmed atrocity together is intentionally upsetting, and rather than making evil comic, it warns against taking refuge—in art or in life—in the objectivity that a satirical perspective can provide. In a similar misconception, Bettelheim omits from his list of reasons for the appearance of Bronzino's picture the irony of its placement in so ugly an environment, or even to consider the more profound problem, about which George Steiner writes, of how the Nazis could have risen from and matured within some of the most sophisticated achievements of Western culture. Bettelheim is saying to Wertmuller: "no matter how talented you are, unless you see the Holocaust as I do, you have no right to treat it (although I cannot stop you if you want to)."

Nonetheless, no amount of self-serving intellectualizing can diminish Wertmuller's achievement. Made from the point of view of a postwar Italian woman, the film proposes that the abuse of her country and its women occurred (and occurs) through the vulgar and violent behavior of an indulged set of thuggish men, some of whom happen to be murderers, who survived the war and learned nothing from the experience. Because of his biases and preferences, Bettelheim is unable to open himself to Wertmuller's themes and her provocative treatment of them.

In addition, Jews appear only peripherally in *Seven Beauties;* on one occasion we see a small group of them being prepared for slaughter in the forest. Their appearance, although brief, shows that they have the filmmaker's respect although not her complete attention. In a way, they represent the side of the Holocaust that Bettelheim would have preferred Wertmuller to treat tragically. The comic treatment is represented by the "charming" survivor Pasqualino, and all those like him, who succumb to evil through a strategy of bluff evasion and criminal activity, and who have neither the caring insight nor the moral sense to know that they have purchased their continuance at the cost of their souls.

II

Many lessons drawn from the Holocaust experience have been urged upon us over the last generation. Theologians, politicians, historians, social critics, and playwrights, among others, have reached conclusions that ask us to accept their advice about issues as diverse as the proper way to create a Jewish identity, the problems in Jewish-Christian and Jewish-Moslem relationships, the dangers and opportunities of political alliances, the existence and nature of God, the price to pay for survival, the intractable prevalence of anti-Semitism, and the importance and methodology of ethical education for children. It seems that no field of human endeavor is exempt from having applied to it some lesson extracted from the Holocaust. So, a curious condition has arisen: in contemporary thought, the Holocaust has become the inexhaustable repository for evidence that can confirm or deny nearly every political, social, or religious attitude.

My own contact with the literature and history of the Holocaust confirms the difficulty in reconciling divergent views of writers who argue with insight and ardor for some program or other. The lessons I draw are not so sweeping, and (unlike Bettelheim) my contact has made me a more wary and skeptical critic. I continue to confront the insolubility of the problems raised by the Holocaust. As Elie Wiesel has remarked, "only the questions can be shared."[12]

The dramas of the Holocaust share these questions and will continue to do so; they are questions of universal and enduring significance. The art of the theatre presents those dramas with the immediacy and provocativeness inherent in live performance. In production, some plays will succeed and others fail, and the reasons why will be complex, perhaps mysterious, but, one hopes, never accidental.[13]

The lessons of the Holocaust are many, and, taken together, are often confusing and contradictory. But, for the most excellent reasons, we should not be deterred from asking questions that have no certain answers. We want to ponder what cannot be fully known and to feel what cannot (and should not) be fully felt. The best Holocaust drama, acknowledging the tension between recollection and forgetting, between performance and audience, confronts with skill, memory and courage the darkness we carry in ourselves into the future. "The holes of oblivion," wrote Hannah Arendt, "do not exist. Nothing human is that perfect, and there are simply too many people in the world to make oblivion possible. One man will always be alive to tell the story."[14]

Notes
Index

Notes

CHAPTER ONE: CHOICE AND/OR SURVIVAL

1. Bruno Bettelheim, "Individual and Mass Behavior in Extreme Situations," in *Surviving and Other Essays* (New York: Knopf, 1979), p. 83.

2. Bruno Bettelheim, "The Holocaust—One Generation After," in *Surviving*, p. 97.

3. Bruno Bettelheim, "The Ignored Lesson of Anne Frank," in *Surviving*, p. 250.

4. See chapter 6, "Responses and Responsibilities," for a fuller discussion of the issues the film raised.

5. Terrence Des Pres, *The Survivor: An Anatomy of Life in the Death Camps* (New York: Oxford University Press, 1976), pp. 87–88.

6. Ibid., p. 128.

7. Terrence Des Pres, "The Bettelheim Problem," *Social Research* 46, no. 4 (Winter 1979): 624. Also see "Us and Them," in *The Survivor*, pp. 149–78.

8. Des Pres, *The Survivor*, p. 129.

9. Bettelheim, "The Ignored Lesson of Anne Frank," p. 247.

10. Bruno Bettelheim, "Eichmann: The System, the Victims," in *Surviving*, p. 270.

11. George Steiner, "Postscript," in *Language and Silence: Essays on Language, Literature, and the Inhuman* (New York: Atheneum, 1967), pp. 166, 167.

12. Sidra DeKoven Ezrahi, *By Words Alone: The Holocaust in Literature* (Chicago: University of Chicago Press, 1980), p. 68.

13. Ibid., p. 69.

14. Lawrence Langer, *Versions of Survival: The Holocaust and the Human Spirit* (Albany: State University of New York Press, 1982), p. 47.

15. Ibid., p. 28.

16. Ibid., pp. 64–65.

17. Ibid., p. 72. In writing of the "death guilt" of survivors, Robert Lifton comments that no survivor of the concentration camps "could be totally unaffected by a pervasive 'either-you-or-me' atmosphere." Robert J. Lifton, *Death in Life* (New York: Random House, 1967), p. 490.

18. Andrej Wirth, "A Discovery of Tragedy," *Polish Review* 12, no. 3 (Summer 1967): 45–46. Sidra Ezrahi's comments on Borowski are found in chapter 3 of *By Words Alone*, pp. 49–66. Langer's appears in chapter 2 of *Versions of Survival*, pp. 67–129.

19. Christopher Hampton, *George Steiner's The Portage to San Cristobal of A.H.* (London: Faber and Faber, 1981). I discuss the play at length in chapter 4. Elie Wiesel was also among the first to identify this phenomenon in his autobiographical memoir *Night* (1958) and later in an essay called "The Guilt We Share," in *Legends Of Our Time* (New York: Holt, Rinehart and Winston, 1968). He describes the devastating psychological condition that is produced in the surviving victim of "choiceless choice."

> Only the number, only the quota counts. Thus, the one who had been spared, above all during the selections, could not repress his first spontaneous reflex of joy. A moment, a week, or an eternity later, this joy weighted with fear and anxiety will turn into guilt. *I am happy to have escaped death* becomes equivalent to admitting: *I am glad that someone* else went in my place. (p. 172)

20. Robert Skloot, ed., *The Theatre of the Holocaust* (Madison: University of Wisconsin Press, 1982), p. 14.

21. Ellen Schiff, *From Stereotype to Metaphor: The Jew in Contemporary Drama* (Albany: State University of New York Press, 1982), p. 210.

22. George Steiner, "A Season in Hell," in *In Bluebeard's Castle: Some Notes Toward the Redefinition of Culture* (New Haven: Yale University Press, 1971), p. 46.

23. Elie Wiesel, *The Town Beyond the Wall*, trans. Stephen Becker (New York: Atheneum, 1964), pp. 67–68.

24. See Lawrence L. Langer, "The Americanization of the Holocaust on Stage and Screen," in *From Hester Street to Hollywood,* ed. Sarah Blacher Cohen (Bloomington: Indiana University Press, 1983), pp. 213–30.

25. Ezrahi, *By Words Alone,* p. 4.

26. Rumkowski has been the subject of much investigation in recent years, by artists as well as historians. He appears as the protagonist of Leslie Epstein's novel *King of the Jews* (1979), and as the central figure in a documentary film *The Story of Chiam Rumkowski and the Jews of Lodz* (1984). Also see Lucjan Dobroszycki, ed., *The Chronicle of the Lodz Ghetto, 1941–1944* (New Haven: Yale University Press, 1984), and Saul Bellow's novel, *Mr. Sammler's Planet* (New York: Viking, 1964).

27. Langer, *Versions,* p. 60.

28. David Roskies, *Against the Apocalypse: Responses to Catastrophe in Modern Jewish Culture* (Cambridge: Harvard University Press, 1984), p. 9.

CHAPTER TWO: TRAGEDY AND THE HOLOCAUST

1. George Steiner, *The Death of Tragedy* (New York: Knopf, 1961), p. 4.

2. George Steiner, "A Kind of Survivor," in *Language and Silence: Essays on Language, Literature, and the Inhuman* (New York: Atheneum, 1967), p. 141.

3. George Steiner, "A Season In Hell," in *In Bluebeard's Castle: Some Notes Toward the Redefinition of Culture* (New Haven: Yale University Press, 1971), p. 30.

4. Richmond Y. Hathorn, *Tragedy, Myth and Mystery* (Bloomington: Indiana University Press, 1962), p. 30.

5. See for example, Robert Alter, "Deformations of the Holocaust," *Commentary* (February 1981): 48–54.

6. Stephen Spender, Introduction to *Selected Poems of Abba Kovner and Nellie Sachs* (Harmondsworth, England: Penguin Books, 1971), p. 7.

7. Terrence Des Pres, *The Survivor* (New York: Oxford University Press, 1976), pp. 9–10.

8. Lawrence L. Langer, *Versions of Survival: The Holocaust and the Human Spirit* (Albany: State University of New York Press, 1982), p. 21.

9. There are, of course, many plays that focus on the actions of heroic Christians such as Raoul Wallenberg, Maximillian Kolbe, or (in Hochhuth's *The Deputy*) Kurt Gerstein, but they are not the subject of my interest here.

10. Wylie Sypher, *Loss of the Self in Modern Literature and Art* (New York: Vintage Books, 1962), p. 14.

11. Sidra DeKoven Ezrahi, *By Words Alone: The Holocaust in Literature* (Chicago: University of Chicago Press, 1980), pp. 8, 9.

12. "Because we, the readers, know what happened after their [the playwrights'] last line was written, the tragic spirit of the text is implicit and we are obliged to complete the tale . . . We must remember that we are posterity, the future generation to whom this testimony was addressed under penalty of death." Ellen S. Fine, "Surviving Voice: Literature of the Holocaust," in *Perspectives on the Holocaust,* ed. Randolph L. Braham (Boston: Kluwer-Nijoff, 1983), p. 110.

13. Eric Bentley, *The Life of the Drama* (New York: Atheneum, 1967), p. 147.

14. See Lawrence L. Langer, "The Americanization of the Holocaust on Stage and Screen," in *From Hester Street to Hollywood,* ed. Sarah Blacher Cohen (Bloomington: Indiana University Press, 1983), pp. 213–230.

15. Robert J. Lifton, *Death in Life* (New York: Random House, 1967), p. 475.

16. Walter Kerr, *Tragedy and Comedy* (New York: Simon and Schuster, 1967), pp. 271–72.

17. Michael K. Brady, *Korczak's Children,* in manuscript version, available from the author. The play premiered at Boston College in 1983.

18. Langer, "The Americanization of the Holocaust," p. 214. James Rosenberg has written:

> The real problem for American playwrights and directors and
> actors has been, not that they have refused to learn the lessons of
> the master, in a technical sense, but that they have been unwilling
> to pay the price of the lesson in tears and suffering and humiliation.

The history of the American nation has been one of avoidance of experience—particularly any painful or upsetting experience. But this, needless to say, is a dangerously immature attitude, and out of it no very profound or useful insights can be expected to develop.

"European Influences" in *American Theatre,* ed. J. R. Brown and B. Harris (London: Edward Arnold, 1967), p. 64.

19. Richard B. Sewell, "The Tragic Form," in *Tragedy: Modern Essays in Criticism* (Englewood Cliffs, N.J.: Prentice-Hall, 1963), pp. 128–29.

20. Charlotte Delbo, *Who Will Carry the Word?* in *The Theatre of the Holocaust,* ed. Robert Skloot (Madison: University of Wisconsin Press, 1982), p. 325.

21. Liliane Atlan, *Monsieur Fugue ou le mal de terre* (Paris: Editions du Seuil, 1967). The play is available in English translation by Marguerite Feitlowitz from the Penkevill Publishing Co., Greenwood, Fla., 32443.

22. In Skloot, *The Theatre of the Holocaust,* pp. 197–265.

23. Ibid., pp. 39–112.

24. See Isaiah Trunk's *Judenrat: The Jewish Councils in Eastern Europe Under Nazi Occupation* (New York: Macmillan, 1972) and Raul Hilberg's newly revised *The Destruction of the European Jews* (New York: Holmes and Meier, 1985), 3 vols.

25. In Skloot, *The Theatre of the Holocaust,* pp. 113–196.

26. Joshua Sobol, *Ghetto,* trans. Miriam Shlesinger (Tel Aviv: Institute for the Translation of Hebrew Literature, 1986). The play premiered in 1984. Much of the historical material about Gens is found in Leonard Tushnet's book, *The Pavement of Hell* (New York: St. Martin's Press, 1972), which describes the parallel careers of three ghetto leaders: Gens (Vilna), Rumkowski (Lodz) and Adam Czerniakow (Warsaw). Four specific incidents in Sobol's play are also narrated in Tushnet's account. Interviews with resistance fighters from the ghetto in Josh Waletzky's excellent 1987 film *The Partisans of Vilna* present a sympathetic picture of Gen's leadership.

27. See Tushnet, *Pavement,* pp. 169–70, where some of this speech is to be found word for word. In the foreword to the book, Tushnet writes: "Tragedy in art gives understanding of man's strivings and failings as well as catharsis. We know what will happen to Oedipus and yet we follow the play with mounting terror as the inexcusable workings of his destiny unfold. We try to comprehend what strengths and weaknesses brought him to his blind end. Putting aside all prejudice, we should seek to understand why Rumkowski, Czerniakow, and Gens did what they did" (p. xi).

28. Langer, *Versions,* p. 128.

CHAPTER THREE: THE (TRAGI)COMIC VISION

1. Walter Kerr, *Tragedy and Comedy* (New York: Simon and Schuster-Clarion, 1968), p. 22. Chapter 2 is called "The Tragic Source of Comedy."

2. Quoted by Robert Corrigan in his Introduction to *Comedy: Meaning and Form* (San Francisco: Chandler Publishing Co., 1965), p. 9. Early in the 1980s, Ionesco wrote the libretto for an opera about Maximillian Kolbe, the Catholic priest who gave up his life to save a Polish prisoner in Auschwitz. See *Maximillian Kolbe,* trans. Rosette Lamont, *Performing Arts Journal* 17 (1982): 32–36.

3. Corrigan, "Comedy and the Comic Spirit, in *Comedy,* p. 6.

4. Susanne Langer, "The Comic Rhythm," in Corrigan, *Comedy,* p. 140.

5. Northrop Frye, "The Mythos of Spring: Comedy," in Corrigan, *Comedy,* p. 155.

6. Eric Bentley, *The Life of the Drama* (New York: Atheneum, 1967), p. 298.

7. Martin Esslin, *The Theatre of the Absurd* (Garden City, N.Y.: Doubleday Anchor Books, 1961), p. 133.

8. David L. Hirst, *Tragicomedy* (London: Methuen, 1984), p. xi.

9. Bentley, *The Life of the Drama,* p. 336.

10. In his study *The Dark Comedy: The Development of Modern Comic Tragedy,* J. L. Styan writes:

> Thus tragedy "in the full sense of the word" is missing today. Our present day mongrel convention, interbred with the spirit of naturalism, can better do other things, and do not encourage the exclusive consistency of purpose we ask of tragedy. Twentieth-century currents of contradictory thought and the mood of audiences do not permit it; the laws of tragedy belong to a world which is religious in its affirmation of human greatness. . . . In an age when tragedy is submerged in moral indifference, we may expect a kind of tragicomedy to come into its own. (Cambridge: Cambridge University Press, 1968), 2d ed., p. 36.

11. For fuller expressions of these ideas, see Lawrence Langer, *The Holocaust and the Literary Imagination* (New Haven: Yale University Press, 1975) and Lawrence Langer, *Versions of Survival: The Holocaust and the Human Spirit* (Albany: State University of New York Press, 1982). Also, Irving Howe briefly summarizes much of the argument in "Writing and the Holocaust," *New Republic,* 27 October 1986, pp. 27–39.

12. Bentley, *The Life of the Drama,* p. 353.

13. Millard Lampell, *The Wall* (New York: Samuel French, n.d.) This is the text of the 1964 Arena Stage production as revised from its 1960 original.

14. In Robert Skloot, ed., *The Theatre of the Holocaust* (Madison: University of Wisconsin Press, 1982).

15. Lampell, *The Wall,* p. 99, in a production note appended to the text of this edition. The text, importantly, does conclude with the suffocation of the baby by its mother, Rutka, so that its crying would not attract the Nazi soldiers outside the bunker. In the 1960 version, the baby remained alive, thus assuring

for the play a gain in optimism but a loss in credibility. Lawrence Langer discusses the incident in "The Americanization of the Holocaust on Stage and Screen," in *From Hester Street to Hollywood*, ed. Sarah Blacher Cohen (Bloomington: Indiana University Press, 1983), pp. 219–20.

16. Mark Shechner, "Woody Allen: The Failure of the Theraputic," in Cohen, *From Hester Street to Hollywood*, p. 233.

17. Ibid., p. 234.

18. S. Langer, "The Comic Rhythm," p. 133.

19. C. P. Taylor, *Good* (London: Methuen, 1981), no pagination.

20. Michael Novak and Moshe Waldoks, eds., *The Big Book of Jewish Humor* (New York: Harper Colophon, 1981), p. xiv.

21. The text of the play was obtained from the author, a professor of theatre at the University of Oklahoma in Norman, Oklahoma. For further information, contact the author's agent, Flora Roberts, Inc., 157 West 57th Street, New York, N.Y. 10019. The first fully staged production appeared at the Williamstown Theatre Festival, August 1987.

22. Leo Rosten in *The Joys of Yiddish* lists the many characteristics of the shlemiehl figure, of which the following apply to Kurtzik: foolish, unlucky, submissive, excluded, ineffective, and gullible. My point is that the basis for Kurtzik's character is a comic type that will be modified in the course of the play.

23. Bentley, *The Life of the Drama*, p. 306.

24. The cabaret-vaudeville sketch or form has attracted numerous playwrights of Holocaust drama. Later in this chapter I will discuss two others, Kenneth Bernard and Peter Barnes, but mention should be made of Pip Simmons's horrifying *An Die Musik* produced in London in 1975, and the performance of Peter Weiss's *The Investigation* as a cabaret show in Thomas Schulte-Michels's 1980 Berlin production. For a description of the Simmons work, see Theodore Shank, *"The Pip Simmons Group,"* TDR (December 1975): 41–46. For a description of the Shulte-Michels's production, see the *New York Times*, 7 April 1980, p. 2.

25. Lea Goldberg, *Lady of the Castle*, trans. T. Carmi (Tel Aviv: Institute for the Translation of Hebrew Literature, 1974).

26. Jean-Claude Grumberg, *The Workroom*, American version by Daniel A. Stern with Sara O'Connor (New York: Samuel French, 1982).

27. Glenda Abramson's rich discussion of the play fully addresses the Ibsenesque influences. See "The Plays of the Holocaust," in *Modern Hebrew Drama* (New York: St. Martin's Press, 1979), pp. 116–125.

28. Eugene Ionesco, *Notes and Counter Notes*, trans. Donald Watson (New York: Grove Press, 1964), pp. 26–27.

29. The manuscript of *How We Danced While We Burned* was obtained from the playwright, a professor of English at the Brooklyn Center of Long Island University. The play's only production was at Antioch College in 1973.

30. Peter Barnes, *Laughter!* (London: Heinemann, 1978).

31. Bernard was influenced in writing the play by Jean-François Steiner's *Treblinka,* especially Steiner's frequent use of theatrical metaphors to describe his experience in the camp. The epigraph to the play is from Steiner: ". . . Treblinka has become a theatre, the ring a stage, the prisoners spectators."

32. In the Introduction to his play *Leonardo's Last Supper,* Barnes writes: "And so the aim is to create, by means of soliloquy, rhetoric, formalized ritual, slapstick, songs and dances, a comic theatre of contrasting moods and opposites, where everything is simultaneously tragic and ridiculous. . . . Nothing a writer can imagine is as surrealistic as the reality. Everything has happened. The difficulty is finding the record of it." In *Collected Plays* (London: Heinemann, 1981), p. 122.

33. Bernard Dukore has compared *Auschwitz* and *Good* in his essay "People Like You and Me: The Auschwitz Plays of Peter Barnes and C. P. Taylor," but its usefulness is somewhat diminished because he uses Barnes's play to devalue Taylor's. In the process, he is forced into some critical comparisons that show neither play to best advantage. In *Essays in Theatre* 3, no. 2 (May 1985): 108–24.

CHAPTER FOUR: REVISIONS AND REVERSALS

1. Alvin H. Rosenfeld in *Imagining Hitler* writes: "Indeed, there can be no imaginative apprehension of Hitler today without a concurrent imagining of the Jew." (Bloomington: Indiana University Press, 1985), p. 108.

I am greatly indebted to Rosenfeld's analysis of the postwar explosion in the cultural manifestations of the image of Hitler. I intend my remarks to extend his observations into the theatrical arena and to amplify upon "the popular motif of the Nazi-Jew doppelgänger" (p. 96).

2. Michael Cristofer, *Black Angel* (New York: Dramatists Play Service, 1984). The play premiered in Los Angeles in 1978 and had its New York debut in 1982.

3. I have in mind here such plays as Martin Sherman's *Bent* (discussed in chapter 6) and Joan Shenkar's *The Last of Hitler.*

4. Saul Friedländer, *Reflections of Nazism: An Essay on Kitsch and Death,* trans. Thomas Weyr (New York: Harper and Row, 1984), p. 107. My italics. The problem is also discussed concerning film, pp. 76–77.

5. Sidra DeKoven Ezrahi, *By Words Alone: The Holocaust in Literature* (Chicago: University of Chicago Press, 1980), p. 40.

6. Rosenfeld, *Imagining Hitler,* p. 74.

7. The problem of interpretation is perhaps greatest in the theatre, but curiously the theatre is the place where it can be most easily tested and at least partially solved. This occurs because although many interpretations of a great play are *possible,* a good production makes clear choices about what the text *intends for that moment.* That is why bad productions are those by directors who refuse to make choices, whereas wrong productions are those where inter-

pretive choices seem to contradict the explicit meanings of a text (exploitation) and that are, as a result, incoherent stylistically, thematically, or structurally. Here I assume, as do most critics who apply a "moral" as well as an aesthetic standard to dramatic production, that decisions concerning interpretation can be made, with some being discarded while others prevail. See chapter 6 for a further discussion of this issue. Catherine Itzin, after describing the Pip Simmons Theatre Group's 1975 theatre piece on the Holocaust, *An Die Musik,* cites an anecdote that makes this point:

> Then the audience watched the camp prisoners perform three pieces of music (the Schubert of title, a Liszt, and Beethoven's "Hymn to Joy") at the whip-command of a sadistic SS officer who brutalised and humiliated them—beating them, making them beat each other, beating the rhythms of the music on a woman's bare breasts, and finally gassing them while they played away. In this case the ambiguity was alienating and much too open to misinterpretation: for example, that the material was anti-semitic instead of —as it was no doubt intended—critical of anti-semitism. Certainly it recalled the Jew who paid a lot of money for a crudely anti-semitic engraving in the Portobello Market to prevent it from falling into the hands of someone who might enjoy it.

In *Stages in the Revolution: Political Theatre in Britain Since 1968* (London: Eyre Methuen, 1980), p. 75.

8. Ellen Schiff, *From Stereotype to Metaphor: The Jew in Contemporary Drama* (Albany: State University of New York Press, 1982), p. 208.

9. Of course, *any* theatrical form can be used to achieve these effects. See chapter 5 and the discussion of Kipphardt's *Brother Eichmann* for the way a "documentary" play form can be used for identical purposes. Sidra Ezrahi noted that, in the work of certain documentary playwrights (among whom Kipphardt can be counted) "a kind of interchangeability between victim and victimizer . . . serves to exonerate the historical actors of unique responsibility." In *By Words Alone,* p. 113.

10. In Stanley Eveling, *The Balachites* and *The Strange Case of Martin Richter* (London: Caldar and Boyars, 1970).

11. René Kalisky, *Jim the Lionhearted,* trans. David Willinger and Luc Denevlin, in *An Anthology of Contemporary Belgian Plays: 1970–1982* (Troy, N.Y.: Whitston Publishing Co., 1984). The anthology also contains Kalisky's *Dave on the Beach.*

12. David Willinger, Introduction to *Jim the Lionhearted* in *Anthology,* p. 296.

13. Kalisky, *Jim the Lionhearted,* in *Anthology,* p. 302.

14. Ellen Schiff is more generous to Kalisky's play than I, finding a general idea behind *Jim* that, though plausible, impresses me as too positive for so anti-intellectual a text. She writes: "Still there is no need to document the bewitchment exercised by the Third Reich on multitudes of disaffected, disenchanted

human beings. Kalisky's play posits that the appeal of such identity-conferring ideologies is far from attenuated." In *From Stereotype to Metaphor,* p. 195.

15. Willinger, Introduction to *Jim the Lionhearted* in *Anthology,* p. 297.

16. Robert Shaw, *The Man in the Glass Booth* (New York: Grove Press, 1968).

17. See Barnes's review on 27 September 1968 and Kerr's on 27 August 1967 and 6 October 1968. The 1975 film of Shaw's play, with a screenplay by Edward Anhalt and starring Maximillian Schell considerably alters the original text but preserves all of its confusion. It is a surprisingly inept piece of work with a highly eccentric and distracting performance by Schell.

18. Sidra Ezrahi quotes from a 1966 interview with the German playwright Peter Weiss (whose *The Investigation,* discussed in chapter 5, also deals with the confusion of identities between Nazis and Jews): "I see Auschwitz as a scientific instrument that could have been used by anyone. For that matter, given a different deal, the Jews could have been on the side of the Nazis. They too could have been exterminators." In *By Words Alone,* p. 39.

19. Christopher Hampton, *George Steiner's The Portage to San Cristobal of A.H.* (London: Faber and Faber, 1983). The play had its American premiere at the Hartford Stage Company, in December 1982. For a description of a very different kind of production of *Portage* done in 1986 at the Cleveland Playhouse, see James Leverett, "Going Too Far, Part 2: Political Excesses," *American Theatre* (September 1986): 30–31.

20. See, for negative examples: Hyam Maccoby, "George Steiner's 'Hitler,'" *Encounter* (May 1982): 27–34; Morris Dickstein, "Alive and 90 in the Jungles of Brazil," *New York Times Book Review,* 2 May 1982, pp. 13, 21; and Stefan Kanfer, "The Perversity of G.S.," *New Republic,* 21 April 1982, pp. 35–36. Two favorable assessments are: Bernard Bergonzi, "The Return of the Führer," *TLS,* 12 June 1981, p. 660, and especially Robert Boyers, "Steiner's Holocaust: Politics and Theology," *Salmagundi* (Winter-Spring 1985): 25–49. Alvin H. Rosenfeld's thoughtful evaluations, "Steiner's Hitler," *Salmagundi* (Spring-Summer 1981): 160–74 and in *Imagining Hitler,* pp. 83–102, are also worth reading.

21. Maccoby, "George Steiner's 'Hitler,'" p. 29.

22. "Who Do You Think *You* Are Kidding, Dr. Gilbert?," London *Times,* 11 March 1982. Also see D. J. R. Bruckner, "Talk with George Steiner," *New York Times Book Review* 2 May 1982.

23. See chapter 2.

24. Olivier Renault D'Allones, *Musical Variations on Jewish Thought,* trans. Judith L. Greenberg (New York: George Braziller, 1984), pp. 72–73.

CHAPTER FIVE: SOME GERMAN VOICES

1. Robert Skloot, ed., *The Theatre of the Holocaust* (Madison: University of Wisconsin Press, 1982), p. 17.

2. Anat Feinberg, "The Jewish Experience and 'Vergangenheits-

bewältigung' in Post-War Austrian Drama," in *Colloquia Germanica* (Bern, Switzerland: Francke Verlag, 1985), 71. Early in her essay, Ms. Feinberg makes clear and important distinctions between Austrian and German perspectives on the Holocaust. She discerns the Austrian turning away from confronting the past as beginning at the end of the 1950s.

3. Erwin Sylvanus, *Dr. Korczak and the Children,* trans. George E. Wellwarth, in *Postwar German Theatre,* ed. Michael Benedikt and George E. Wellwarth (New York: Dutton, 1968).

4. George E. Wellwarth, Introduction to *Postwar German Theatre,* p. xvii. In her Introduction to *Essays on German Theater,* Margaret Herzfeld-Sander lists three dominant issues in German drama over the past decade: "the increasing affluence of middle-class society, a lingering Fascist mentality, and human and social indifference." (New York: Continuum, 1985), p. xxvii. Sylvanus himself enlisted in the Wehrmacht and, after sustaining severe wounds, spent much time in war hospitals recuperating.

5. There are numerous "small" lies in the play concerning the image of Korczak, as when he tells of his service in the German army in World War One when he earned the Iron Cross (scene 17). He was actually a medical officer in a Polish unit. Anat Feinberg notes in "Erwin Sylvanus and the Theatre of the Holocaust" that Sylvanus never intended to write a play that was biographically accurate. In *Studien Zur Dramatik in Der Bundesrepublik Deutschland* (Amsterdam: Rodupi, 1983), pp. 163–75.

6. Eric Bentley, Foreword to *The Storm Over The Deputy* (New York: Grove Press, 1964), p. 8.

7. Rolf Hochhuth, *The Deputy,* trans. Richard and Clara Winston (New York: Grove Press, 1964), p. 32.

8. Walter Kaufmann, *Tragedy and Philosophy* (New York: Doubleday, 1968), p. 329.

9. Ibid., p. 331.

10. Rolf Hochhuth, "Should the Theater Portray the Contemporary World?" in *Essays on German Theater,* ed. Margaret Herzfeld-Sander (New York: Continuum, 1985), p. 268. This interview with Hochhuth was conducted in 1963.

11. See Stuart Parkes, "West German Drama Since the War," in *The German Theatre,* ed. Ronald Hayman (London: Oswald Wolff, 1975), pp. 131–37.

12. Martin Esslin, "'Truth' and Documentation: A Conversation with Rolf Hochhuth," in *Reflections: Essays on Modern Theatre* (New York: Anchor Books, 1971). Also, C. D. Innes, *Modern German Drama* (Cambridge: Cambridge University Press, 1979). Hochhuth quotes Shaw in his epigraph to act 1.

13. C. D. Innes comments: "Hochhuth's premise . . . is thrown into question by the need to make his figures equal to their historical background. Instead of drawing individualized characters, the people of the play are weighted with symbolism to counterbalance the mass anonymity of the death camps . . .

Such mythological status is incompatible with individuality . . ." In *Modern German Drama,* p. 202.

14. Peter Weiss, *The Investigation,* English version by Jon Swan and Ulu Grosbard (New York: Atheneum, 1966), pp. 40–42.

15. Alvin Rosenfeld, *A Double Dying: Reflections on Holocaust Literature* (Bloomington: Indiana University Press, 1980), p. 159.

16. For example, see Barbara Garson, "Final Understanding," a review of a 1979 production, in the *Village Voice,* 7 May 1979. Elizabeth Hardwick's negative assessment of the play and its original New York production, "Auschwitz in New York," is found in a collection of her essays, *Bartleby in Manhattan* (New York: Random House, 1982), pp. 140–49.

17. Peter Weiss, "Notes on the Contemporary Theater," in *Essays on German Theater,* ed. Margaret Herzfeld-Sander (New York: Continuum, 1985), p. 298. This interview with Weiss was conducted in 1963. Compare Weiss's statement with Hochhuth's in no. 10. The term "flattening" is taken from Yehuda Bauer's essay "Whose Holocaust?" in *Midstream* 26, no. 9 (November 1980): 45.

18. Michael Patterson has written: "When the initial excitement over documentary drama faded away, it was soon recognized for what it is, a bankruptcy of the imagination with no real guarantee of an objective viewpoint." *German Theatre Today* (London: Pitman, 1976), p. 3.

19. See the *New York Times* 24 September 1985, 1 November 1985, and 12 November 1985 for stories of the most recent controversy over the play. The reaction in the German press has been collected in *Die Fassbinder-Kontroversie oder Das Ende der Schonzeit,* ed. Heiner Lichtenstein (Athenäum, 1986). Also see Seyla Benhabib, "Rainer Werner Fassbinder's 'Trash, the City and Death': When Allegory Becomes Metaphor," *German Studies Newsletter* (March 1986): 30–35.

20. Denis Calandra, "The Antitheatre of R. W. Fassbinder," in *Ranier Fassbinder: Plays* (New York: Performing Arts Journal Press, 1985), p. 12.

21. Rainer Werner Fassbinder, *Garbage, the City and Death* in *Rainer Werner Fassbinder: Plays,* pp. 170–71.

22. Gerald Rabkin in "The Controversial 1985–86 Theatre Season: A Politics of Reception," *Performing Arts Journal 28,* 10, no. 1 (1986): 12.

23. James Leverett, "Going Too Far, Part 2: Political Excesses," *American Theatre* (September 1986): 30.

24. Rabkin, "The Controversial 1985–86 Theatre Season," p. 15.

25. C. D. Innes, *Modern German Drama,* p. 7. Also see Denis Calandra, *New German Dramatists* (New York: Grove Press, 1983), pp. 148–50.

26. See Gitta Honegger, "The Theatre of Thomas Bernhard," Introduction to Thomas Bernhard, *The President and Eve of Retirement* (New York: Performing Arts Journal Press, 1982), p. 14. Also see Calandra, *New German Dramatists,* p. 148, and the articles collected in the Tyrone Guthrie Theatre program for *Eve of Retirement* (Minneapolis: 1981).

27. Benjamin Henrichs, "Mr. Bernhard and the Germans," *Die Zeit,* 6 July 1979, quoted in the Guthrie Theatre program, p. 29.

28. Peter von Becker, "Irrational Maniacs Do Not Perish," *Theater Heute* 8, August 1979, quoted in the Guthrie Theatre program, p. 33.

29. Peter Demetz assesses the play: "It is an unmitigated disaster that survives only because of audiences eager to see Nazi melodrama in endless variations." *After the Fires* (San Diego: Harcourt Brace Jovanovich, 1986), p. 208.

30. Innes, *Modern German Drama,* p. 173.

31. Heinar Kipphardt, *Bruder Eichmann* (Rowohlt, 1983). The translation used in this discussion was obtained from the publisher's American agent Helen Merrill, and is otherwise uncredited. The English text is a significant abridgment of the original. To date, no American production of the play has been performed. Also see Anat Feinberg, "The Appeal of the Executive: Adolf Eichmann on Stage," *Monatshefte* 78, no. 2 (1986): 203–14.

32. Anson Rabinbach, Introduction to *Germans and Jews Since the Holocaust,* ed. A. Rabinbach and J. Zipes (New York: Holmes and Meier, 1986), p. 5.

33. Innes, *Modern German Drama,* p. 2.

34. Ibid., p. 265, 3. Although not prepared to take up the flag of naturalism, I cannot agree completely with Innes's conclusion that "the naturalistic conventions, which are so suitable for exploring private suffering or exposing the personal deception behind a respectable facade, continually break down in this attempt to deal with the experience of fascism" (p. 22).

CHAPTER SIX: RESPONSES AND RESPONSIBILITIES

1. I discuss the metaphorical problems of dealing with the Holocaust in the Introduction to *The Theatre of the Holocaust* (Madison: University of Wisconsin Press, 1982), pp. 15–16.

2. Peter Demetz, *After the Fires* (San Diego: Harcourt Brace Jovanovich, 1986), p. 22.

3. Martin Sherman, *Bent* (New York: Avon, 1980).

4. Ibid., pp. 77–80. A more recent book on this subject is Richard Plant, *The Pink Triangle: The Nazi War Against Homosexuals* (New York: Henry Holt, 1986).

5. Lawrence Langer, *Versions of Survival* (Albany: State University of New York Press, 1982), p. 46.

6. Bruno Bettelheim, "Surviving," in *Surviving and Other Essays* (New York: Knopf, 1979), pp. 274–314. Des Pres's angry response to Bettelheim's attack on him is found in "The Bettelheim Problem," *Social Research* 46, no. 4 (Winter 1979): 619–47. He comments: "I shall not waste time discussing the film, nor question Bettelheim's interpretation, except to say that he plainly puts no stock in the idea of art as *criticism of life,* but rather clings to the Romantic notion that the protagonist, simply by virtue of occupying center stage, carries the endorsement of the artist and audience . . ." (p. 636).

7. Bettelheim, *Surviving,* p. 280, 281.

8. Ibid., p. 281.

9. Ibid., p. 282.

10. Ibid., p. 300.

11. Here I disagree with Des Pres in his suggestion that Pasqualino changes. See "Bleak Comedies: Lina Wertmuller's Artful Method," *Harpers,* June, 1976. I also dispute the conclusions of Jerzy Kosinski, who, while maintaining that Pasqualino begins and ends a loathsome individual, dismisses him as a "cartoon." See *"Seven Beauties*—A Cartoon Trying to be a Tragedy," *New York Times,* 7 March 1976, sec. 2.

12. Elie Wiesel, "To a Young Jew of Today," in *A Jew Today,* trans. Marion Wiesel (New York: Random House, 1978), p. 175.

13. Susan Sontag has remarked: ". . . an awareness of the reality of evil is the best defense against artistic trivialization and vulgarity." "On Art and Consciousness," *Performing Arts Journal* 2, no. 2 (Fall, 1977): 27.

14. Hannah Arendt, *Eichmann in Jerusalem: A Report on the Banality of Evil,* rev. ed. (New York, Viking Press, 1964), 232–33.

Index

COMPOSED BY THE COMPOSING ROOM, INC., APPLETON, WISCONSIN
MANUFACTURED BY THOMSON-SHORE, INC., DEXTER, MICHIGAN
TEXT AND DISPLAY LINES ARE SET IN SABON

Library of Congress Cataloging-in-Publication Data
Skloot, Robert.
The darkness we carry.
Includes index.
1. Holocaust, Jewish (1939–1945), in literature.
2. Drama—20th century—History and criticism. 3. Jews
in literature. I. Title.
PN1879.H65S58   1988   809.2′9358   87-40376
ISBN 0-299-11660-3
ISBN 0-299-11664-6 (pbk.)